D1451930

THE BOOKS OF
KING HENRY VIII
AND HIS WIVES

THE BOOKS OF
KING HENRY VIII
AND HIS WIVES

JAMES P. CARLEY

PREFACE BY

DAVID STARKEY

THE BRITISH LIBRARY

For J.E.H.

First published in 2004 by
The British Library
96 Euston Road
London NW1 2DB

British Library Cataloguing-in-Publication Data
A catalogue record for this title is available from
the British Library

ISBN 0 7123 4791 7

Designed and typeset in Monotype Poliphilus and Blado italic
by Peter and Alison Guy
Printed in Hong Kong by South Sea International Press

Frontispiece: The British Library, C.18.c.9 front cover

CONTENTS

PREFACE

BY

DAVID STARKEY

Bibliography has, traditionally, been one of the most esoteric scholarly arts. But recently it has moved from the back workshop to the front window. Scholars have become interested in the book as object. They have looked at how it was printed and illustrated. They have also examined how it was used. What notes were written in it? Does it show signs of being read at all?

But James Carley's innovation is different. He looks at the book as property and asks who acquired it and for what purpose. And in this book he asks the question of some of the most important readers and acquirers of all in the Sixteenth Century: Henry VIII and His Six Wives.

These royal readers acquired books, in part, for the simple reason that they were bookish. The king himself and the first and last of his wives, Catherine of Aragon and her namesake and probable god-daughter, Catherine Parr, were highly educated; all three received numerous dedications, while Henry and Catherine Parr were themselves authors. Henry wrote the anti-Lutheran tract, the *Assertio Septem Sacramentorum*; Catherine Parr, *Prayers and Meditations* and *The Lamentations of a Sinner*.

The former was in Latin, was aimed at an international audience and was so ultra-orthodox that it not only won Henry the title of *Fidei Defensor* from a grateful Pope, but also drew the warning from Thomas More, of all people, that Henry might live to regret the high claims for the Papal supremacy which he advanced. Catherine Parr's books, in contrast, were in English and were aimed at the common man or even woman. While their tone ranged from the affectively evangelical in *Prayers and Meditations* to the frankly Lutheran in *Lamentations of a Sinner*, which was published only once Henry, who never wavered in his hostility to Luther, was safely dead. And *Lamentations* is not only Lutheran, but openly, even vehemently anti-Papist.

And it is the contrast within this trio of royal books, the first published in the 1520s and the second pair in the 1540s, which take us to the heart of the matter. For both positions, Henry's extreme Papalism and Catherine's evangelism or Lutheranism (which was equally extreme in its way), were products of learning and bookish argument. To get from one to the other required a battle of the books. We are familiar with the idea that the Reformation was fought with the printing press. But the idea that libraries were equally tools of religious warfare is more novel. First sketched by Tom Birrell in his seminal Panizzi Lectures, 'English Monarchs and their Books', it was fully developed by James Carley himself in an astonishing series of learned articles that culminated in his magisterial *The Libraries of King Henry VIII*. This shorter book is a distillation of these riches of scholarship; its tone is more emphatically biographical and it complements the study of Henry's books with those of his queens.

For, arguably, it was the queens who mattered most, in Henry's bibliography as in his biography. This holds true even for the books that Henry inherited from his English royal ancestors. These, together with his own substantial acquisitions, were displayed by Henry's father, Henry VII, in a purpose-built library in his favourite palace at Richmond. And the king showed them, with all the joy and pride of ownership, to a pensive Catherine of Aragon shortly after her marriage to Prince Arthur in November 1501. Henry, then a boisterous ten-year-old, was a member of the party; but it was Catherine, six years older and with an equal if not superior education to her future husband, who would have appreciated them most.

Books seem to have figured little during Catherine's first, brief marriage to Arthur, or in the locust years which followed. But, once she was married to Henry, they would stand side by side in the battle of the books against Lutheranism, just as they had jointly taken on the French and their Scottish allies in the first wars of the reign. For Henry's *Assertio* is complemented by two anti-Lutheran works by Catherine's confessor; both are dedicated to her and one asserts that she often discussed the problem with her spiritual adviser.

But this partnership came to an abrupt end when Henry fell passionately in love with Anne Boleyn in 1526-7. Here Carley's contribution is of the first importance. He shows how Henry accumulated a working library (as opposed to his father's display library at Richmond) to enable him and his researchers to formulate the theological and legal arguments against his first marriage. But Henry only began to acquire such a library in 1529. This means that Henry fell in love adulterously first and only then cast around for arguments to justify his divorce. Even more important is the evidence of Anne Boleyn's own books. These demonstrate, beyond argument, that she was a convinced Evangelical, even (as the Imperial ambassador, Chapuys, insisted) a Lutheran. This implies in turn that she was not simply the occasion of religious change, but its acting, shaping agent.

Finally, above and beyond politics, Carley's book bears witness to a central cultural change. The books of Henry's father, Henry VII, and his grandfather, Edward IV, were large, ostentatious and designed to be read aloud; Henry, in contrast, as an illustration in his *Psalter* shows, read books in an arm-chair in the comfort of his bed chamber; while his greatest subject, the duke of Norfolk, went further and, as he explained, could only get to sleep if he had a book to read in bed. Reading, in other words, had changed from a public to a private activity and, as it did so, the real age of the book began. The change, moreover, not only took place in Henry's reign, the king and his wives, whether as readers, writers or collectors of books, played a key role in it.

Read this book and see!

AUTHOR'S NOTE

'So clear an example of strict and harmonious wedlock'
Erasmus to Henry VIII, 1519

Several years ago, when I was preparing an edition of the inventories of
King Henry VIII's libraries for the Corpus of British Medieval Library Catalogues series, I vaguely imagined a companion volume, one that would be
fully illustrated and more user-friendly. The typescript in due course delivered
to the publishers, I turned to my principal scholarly endeavour – editions and
studies of the remains of the Tudor antiquary John Leland – for which all
four hundred pages of the *The Libraries of King Henry VIII* had stood as a pro-
legomenon. After *The Libraries* appeared in print I was flattered when one
reader, admittedly a bibliographer, assured me that he had read the tome from
cover to cover. His reaction also brought to mind my earlier lamentations and
raised the possibility of a discursive rather than descriptive volume: one with
visual component. But I was also slightly concerned. Was this what I should be
doing? Was it yet another excuse to put off Leland, who has been weighing on
my conscience for some twenty years? In the end I succumbed – feeling rather
guilty, as one does in such circumstances – and as I was putting the finishing
touches on my text, there was a sign, a bit of synchronicity, which convinced
me that I had been right in my instincts.

One Sunday morning in Oxford in the autumn of 2002 – Duke Humfrey
and the autograph manuscript of Leland's *De uiris illustribus* not being available – I was working on the section concerning Henry's wives, hoping to
make it clear that the development of Henry's libraries must be linked to his
marital adventures and their unhappy outcomes. Normally, I don't watch television, but feeling rather gloomy I decided to see if there was any news – the
world situation, I reckoned, would make my own lot (lonely and far from
home) seem positively rosy. Instead I got *My Favourite Hymns*. The guest of the
day was the musician Rick Wakeman, who was describing a dream he had
had about the beheading of Anne Boleyn while he was recording his 1973
album on *The Six Wives of Henry VIII*. In the dream Wakeman was himself
a witness to the execution: after the headsman finished his appointed task, the
assembled crowd spontaneously broke into song with a tearful rendering of
'The Day Thou Gavest, Lord, Is Ended'. I suspect that my own unconscious
might have dredged up a different hymn from this – although there is a grim
irony in the line 'The darkness falls at thy behest' – but the slightly disconcert-
ing juxtaposition of worlds, scholarly and musical, computer and television
screen, did convince me that writing this book must have been part of my des-
tiny. Certainly it has been an immense pleasure and I am deeply grateful to all
the colleagues and friends who have given me assistance: David Starkey, who
allowed me access to the typescript of his *Six Wives: The Queens of Henry VIII*
before its publication; David Way, who cajoled me into undertaking the project;
Janet Backhouse, Peter Barber, Anne Barton, Meg Bent, Tom Birrell, Peter

Blayney, Alixe Bovey, Claire Breay, David Carlson, Jeremy Catto, Georgina Difford, Ted Dumitrescu (who rescued me from several musicological blunders), Tom Freeman, Maria Hayward, Ann Hutchison, William Kemp, Simon Keynes, Diarmaid MacCulloch, Giles Mandelbrote, David McKitterick (who drew my attention to the royal copy of the *Pylgrimage of Perfection*) and to Nicholas Poole-Wilson (who located it for me), Richard Rex, Felicity Riddy, Richard Sharpe, Frank Stubbings, and Mary Beth Winn. Colin Tite, James Willoughby and Jonathan Woolfson have pored over the text, making stimulating suggestions as well as saving me from infelicities great and small: as on previous occasions I am much indebted to all three. Parts of this book formed the basis for my Sir Lionel Denny Lecture at the Museum of London in 1998 and for my Deneke Lecture at Lady Margaret Hall, Oxford, in 1999.

More than a decade ago the Canadian novelist Robertson Davies presented me with a wax impression taken, so he assured me, from St Dunstan's seal. When I queried its authenticity he fixed me with a powerful stare and stated: 'That is the trouble with you academics; narrow-minded and reductionist. With all your facts you often miss the essential truth of the past'. Over the years I have handled many books owned by Henry as well as his wives and, somewhat chastened by Rob, I have let them speak to me rather than trying to pin them down to a specific meaning. And they have had much to say; not only through marginalia – some of which have been provocatively revealing – but also because of their status as relics, material links with great names of the past. Rarely, if ever, have I opened a Henrician book (and in this term I include books associated with his wives and courtiers) without a shiver of anticipation and excitement; rarely have I closed one without having learnt something new.

After much consideration of the pros and cons I decided not to use footnotes in the present volume, taking my inspiration from Tom Birrell's highly successful Panizzi lectures on *English Monarchs and their Books*, which concluded with the following statement: 'The anecdotal nature of these lectures has been both deliberate and inevitable. I can only hope to have conveyed something of the intellectual excitement that I have felt as I have explored the heterogeneous mixture of riches and dross that makes up what has survived of the Royal Library.' In cases where the sources of my statements are readily accessible I have simply assumed that the interested reader can trace the material without difficulty. In my 'Further Reading' section I have, however, included references to pertinent books and articles containing more detailed discussions.

I dedicated *The Libraries of King Henry VIII* to Eric and Elspeth Hutchison, who for many years provided me with accommodation and fostering in Cambridge. In Toronto Janet Hutchison, Eric's sister, has done no less for me. She (and her cheque book) have egged me on every time I felt I needed yet another book relating to the topic – and a very broad topic it has become too. She has given me encouragement and sometimes has nagged too. Whenever I have tried to imagine my ideal reader, her 'shining face' has popped into my mind's eye. To Janet, then, I dedicate this book with warmest affection.

7 January 2004

1. This sammelband contains five short treatises published on the Continent between 1526 and 1536, and bound in a delicately embroidered crimson satin binding. Other of Henry's books also had embroidered bindings, including the presentation copy, now The British Library, Royal MS 20.A.IV, of Martin de Brion's 'Description de toute la terre saincte'. The British Library, C.21.f.14, cover

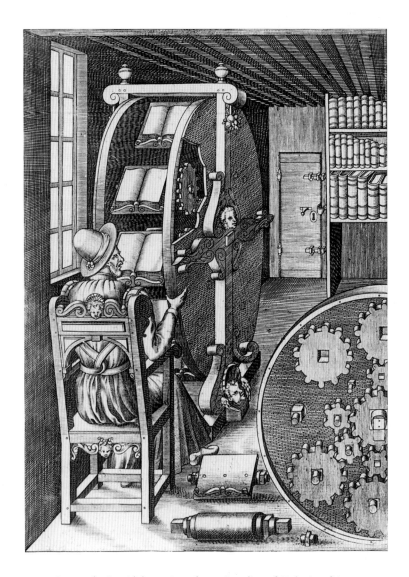

2. In 1531 the Spanish humanist and sometime client of Catherine of Aragon, Juan Luis Vives, commented on the 'uncountable numbers of books' which were being printed and which were causing people to 'moan inwardly, and ask: "Who can read all these?"' One of the solutions proposed was the revolving reading desk, illustrated here in Agostino Ramelli's *Le diverse et artificiose machine* (Paris, 1588). The British Library, 48.f.15, p. 317

HENRY VIII was born in 1491, the year before Christoper Columbus discovered America. A distinctly pious individual, he spent his early years as a loyal son of the Church, but long before his death in 1547 he had broken definitively with Rome. He succeeded his father and entered his first marriage in 1509, the same year as Michelangelo unveiled the Sistine Chapel ceiling. Unlike most of his fellow monarchs he thought love and marriage – as David Starkey has so brilliantly shown – could be combined, and yet he was married six times. Henry VII's claim to the throne may have been a dubious one, but during his son's lifetime the Tudor myth became firmly entrenched in the English consciousness through the writings of historians such as the Italian Polydore Vergil and more literary types such as Sir Thomas More.

Henry's reign witnessed the emergence of England from the Middle Ages and the first real flowering of the new intellectual habit of mind known as humanism in England, the search for models and prototypes in the classical past. In spite of all its turmoil and activity Henry's world was a bookish one and he was a bookish king from beginning to end; so too were fifty per cent of his wives. Henry and the book are as closely intertwined as Henry and politics or Henry and religion, and this topic deserves the same close analysis as the others have received in the past. My study is thus devoted to Henry and his wives as bibliophiles, focusing on the magnificent and revealing collections of books they amassed. Less evidence, not surprisingly, survives concerning the wives and a much smaller proportion of my narra-tive focuses on them. Nevertheless, the books they owned are extraordinarily revealing and provide new insights into the intellectual and emotional lives of most of these women, even though their books, unlike those of their hus-band, normally lack marginalia.

From the time of his first childhood encounter with the renowned humanist Desiderius Erasmus, scholars were uniform in their praise of Henry's learning: as in so much else, the Dutchman set the tone when he professed himself dazzled by the brilliance of the young prince when he was taken to visit the royal children at Eltham Palace in 1499. A few years later, in a Coronation Day poem, Sir Thomas More asked rhetorically (and perhaps somewhat ambiguously): 'what could lie beyond the powers of a prince whose natural gifts have been enhanced by a liberal education, a prince bathed by the nine sisters in the Castalian fount and steeped in philosophy's own precepts?' More also maintained that the young king possessed 'greater erudition and judgment than any previous monarch'. In his *De fructu qui ex doctrina percipitur* (*The Benefit of a Liberal Education*), published in 1517, the diplomat and royal secretary Richard Pace observed that 'we have a most noble king who far surpasses all other Christian princes in learning as well as in power. He is so well disposed to all *eruditi* that he hears nothing more willingly than conversations about scholars and books.' Writing to Henry on 15 May 1519 Erasmus waxed hyperbolic: 'Time was when from a sort of passion for literature and the delights of learned ease I felt some repugnance to the courts of kings. But now, when I contemplate what a prince and gover-nor rules the English court, its queen, its nobles, counsellors, officials, I am eager in spirit to betake myself to a court like that.' Nor did Henry himself have any small estimation of his intellectual prowess: chastising the Yorkshire rebels in 1536 he expressed himself astounded that ignorant folk would take it upon themselves 'to instruct us (which sometimes have been noted to be learned)'.

As well as being receptive to new ideas Henry was a generous patron: William Blount, Lord Mountjoy, assured Erasmus in 1509 that 'Heaven smiles, earth rejoices; all is milk and honey and nectar. Tight-fistedness is well and truly banished. Generosity scatters wealth with unstinting hand.' Given the intellectual tenor of Henry's court, indeed, it is inevitable that scholars flocked to it and that by the end of his reign his libraries were well stocked; apart from the books he had inherited, seized from the dissolved monasteries and sequestered from fallen courtiers and wives, there were up-to-date humanist editions as well as a variety of presentation materials.

Several factors came together to render Henry's reign a key epoch in terms of book history in England and to make his collection, the corner-stone of the modern British Library, such a major one. First, perhaps, was Henry's own love of possession and ostentation. He was a collector *par excellence* and stocked his palaces as grandly as he could. At a time when *belles lettres* were prized as highly as architectural magnificence, it is natural that he would turn to books both for their contents and for their bindings, emulating the fine humanist collection being built up by his 'brother' monarch Francis I of France. (1) His was an age in which books proliferated as a result of the printing press and his libraries expanded at a rate unheard of in earlier generations, in part because so much more was available. (2) The availability of books, however, also raised questions of state control. Unsurprisingly, then, not only was Henry concerned about what he himself might wish to acquire, he also attempted to legislate on what his subjects should be permitted to read.

The floodgates unloosed by the printing press thus highlighted developing religious controversy: dissemination of theological texts, especially biblical translations and commentaries, became a powerful tool in the hands of reformers. Henry's perspective on reform, negative or positive, shifted over the years, as did his view on the suitability of the vernacular Bible for the laity. Nevertheless, throughout his reign, he himself collected Bibles: by the time he died he owned French and English translations as well as versions in Greek, Latin, and Hebrew. Although there is no evidence that Henry could read Hebrew, he was well aware of the importance of the language and in the 1520s encouraged his young cousin Reginald Pole to become familiar with it. In the next decade the eminent continental scholar, Sebastian Münster, dedicated his Hebrew text of St Matthew's Gospel to the king and the presentation copy of John Sheprey's translation of the Epistles of James and Jude into Hebrew still survives in the royal library. Most abundant were manuscript copies of St Jerome's Vulgate, the majority deriving from the dissolved monasteries and many with the standard fivefold glosses dwarfing the actual sacred text. (3) Henry also possessed a goodly number of printed Bibles, including a copy of the Complutensian polyglot Bible, of which only six hundred or so copies were issued. Taking its name from the Latin

3. Some of Henry's Vulgates were beautifully produced, such as this two-volume example written in the Netherlands in 1451, the borders illuminated in the fashionable Flemish manner. It also contains a detached miniature of the Fall, with a portrait of the king and the royal arms in the border.

4. Published in six parts between 1514 and 1517, the Complutensian polyglot Bible represented a technical triumph for the printers with its sophisticated juxtaposition of scripts in parallel columns. Cardinal Ximenes is said to have spent half a million ducats on its production.

The British Library, G11951
(opening of Genesis)

for Alcalá de Henares, where it was published in the university which Cardinal Ximenes had founded in 1510, this is the earliest complete polyglot Bible, containing in parallel columns Hebrew, Greek, Latin, Chaldaic and Aramaic versions of the text. Subsequently abstracted from the royal library, Henry's copy is now to be found in the University Library at St Andrews. (4) Henry owned Erasmus's translation of the New Testament, on which the latter had worked when he was at Cambridge University between 1511 and 1514. Following the ancient father of the church, Tertullian, who viewed the biblical books as documents and sources of argument, Erasmus called his version the *Novum Instrumentum* ('New Record') rather than *Novum Testamentum*, and in it he included his own commentary.

During the period of his infatuation with Anne Boleyn Henry showed himself sympathetic to French evangelical thought and he owned biblical translations into French by the progressively minded scholar Jacques Lefèvre d'Etaples, translations which had been condemned by the theological faculty at the Sorbonne in Paris (frontispiece). Towards the end of Henry's life the Dutch reformer Wouter Deleen became a member of the royal household, occupying the position of 'biblioscopus', that is reader or censor. His Latin edition of the New Testament was published in London in 1540 and was dedicated to the king. (5) Henry received a copy on vellum of the 1539 Great Bible, the first authorized Bible in English, as well as a

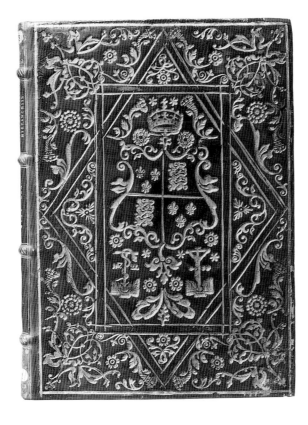

5. The presentation copy of Deleen's *Novum Testamentum latine* is one of the four books, three of them gifts to Henry from Deleen, to have been bound by an individual appropriately called by modern scholars the Flamboyant Binder. Another example of his work, illustrated here, is his unprinted *Libellus de tribus hierarchiis, ecclesiastica, politica, et oeconomica.*
The British Library,
Royal MS 12.B.xiii, cover

copy of the second edition of 1540 in which the illuminator has made copious changes to the woodcut print. According to a handwritten inscription this latter was presented by Anthony Marler, merchant and haberdasher of London, who in 1541 would obtain a licence to sell the Bibles for ten shillings unbound and for twelve shillings bound, 'being trymmed with bullyons [knobs]'. (6) Marler persuaded the Privy Council to issue a 'Proclamation confirming injunctions heretofore set forth by royal authority for curates and parishoners to provide "by a day now expired" and set up in every church, Bibles containing the Old and New Testaments in English'. Even though he was soon afterwards arrested following one of the regular shifts in religious policy – the vernacular Bible also finding itself in trouble with the authorities – Marler had clearly realized the advantages of a captive audience. What this proclamation indicates, too, is just how thoroughly print had replaced manuscript as the official voice of Henry's government by the 1540s, how completely modern the communication network had become. If an inventory of Henry's libraries had been taken at the begin-

6. The illuminator has personalized the woodcut of Henry in this presentation copy of the Great Bible, representing the king with a prominent mouth and full auburn beard as well as showing his imperial robes and closed crown.
The British Library,
C.18.d.10, title page

ning of his reign there would have been relatively few printed books in them; by the end, these would dominate both in quantity and in prestige.

The chapters that follow in Part I document the evolution of the Henrician book collection and show how its transformation mirrored the king's own changing views and policies as well as the technological developments of his lifetime. Henry's collection was never as sophisticated as Francis I's, for example, but in many ways it was a more interesting one and more deeply revealing of the owner's character. When juxtaposed with the books of his wives, as described in Part II, it becomes even more fascinating and we can see how closely his intellectual life converged with his marital adventures; how much, at least in a library context, the heart and mind complemented each other. Especially in the case of his first two marriages, the battle of the wives is reflected in the battle of the books.

7. This chansonnier, which carries the same Westminster inventory number as the Magdalene manuscript, has two miniatures in the Flemish style, this one showing a lady playing an instrument, with a winged figure behind her and the poet offering his tears.
The British Library, Royal MS 20.A.XVI, f. 3v

8. Trunks, chests, coffers and standards would have been used for moving goods. Although this chest dates to a later period, it is similar in both design and construction to those that would have been employed by Henry. Most of the coffers contained clothing, jewellery and other necessities, but some had books, pens, 'yncke potts', and other miscellaneous 'stuff'.

National Trust Photographic Library/Andreas von Einsiedel

THE PHYSICAL SETTING:

STORAGE OF THE TRAVELLING LIBRARY AND

PALACE COLLECTIONS

In his *Description of England*, the Elizabethan historian William Harrison described Henry VIII as 'the onelie Phenix of his time for fine and curious masonrie', and without doubt Henry was a great builder and refurbisher of residences. When he died in 1547 he had more than sixty establishments – some, such as Beddington Place, Surrey (which had been owned by his former favourite Sir Nicholas Carew), seized after treason trials and others, such as Rochester Priory, part of the booty from the dissolved monasteries. For a variety of reasons, including availability of game and sanitation, the court – which on occasion could number close to a thousand people – moved regularly from palace to palace, many of the king's goods travelling with him in appropriate containers. (8) After his death these were stored in the secret Jewel House in the Tower of London: those marked with letters A to X contained the king's travelling goods, those with numbers 1 to 11, the queen's. Some of the books in the coffers must have remained in the Tower long after Henry's death: a surviving copy of the 1536 edition of the Commentary on the Gospels and Epistles by Smaragdus of SaintMihiel (d. *c*.830) now at York Minster, for example, has a note by an unknown individual declaring that 'This booke was founde by me in the Juell House amongstt K. Henrie the 8 his bookes the 22th of November 1600 in the Tower'.

Coffer M contained perhaps the most coherent group: it had documents relating to the restructuring of the church, distribution of church lands and other accounts, valuations predominating. To make perusal easier 'one case of spectacles' was included. Coffer F housed books and writing materials (including a 'wryting candlesticke') in the smaller drawers or 'tills'. Titles indicate that this coffer was devoted to music and surgery. This is not surprising: Henry was highly literate musically and was much commended at home and abroad for this skill. In 1515 Niccolò Sagudino, secretary to the Venetian ambassador, wrote that Henry 'is likewise so gifted and adorned with mental accomplishments of every sort that we believe him to have few equals in the world. He speaks English, French and Latin; understands Italian well; plays on almost every instrument, sings and composes fairly.'

According to an extremely important inventory of Westminster Palace taken in 1542 which included a relatively full account of books in the library, Henry owned a number of music manuscripts, including three lost luting books. He also possessed a beautiful French chansonnier, now in the Pepys Library at Magdalene College Cambridge. Described as a 'pricke songe booke', it contains fiftyseven three and fourvoice sacred and secular pieces in Latin, French and Italian. Probably commissioned for a member

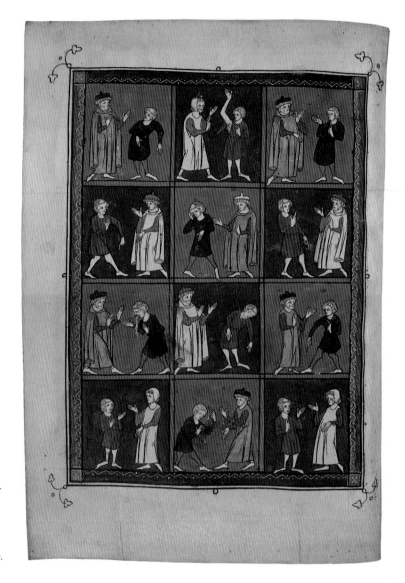

9. Illustrated here are four scenes of
consultation between a doctor and
his ailing patient, who is suffering
from nausea, vertigo, toothache,
and a scalp condition.
The British Library, Sloane MS 1977, f. 50v.

of the French royal family, and then converted into a diplomatic gift, perhaps at the time of Henry's coronation in 1509, this chansonnier stands as a
monument to the musical tastes of the French court and chapel during the
reign of Louis XII. (7) Another manuscript (now Additional Manuscript
31922 in the British Library) contains a number of pieces ascribed to Henry
himself, probably composed in the years soon after his marriage to Catherine
of Aragon, when musical entertainments were very much part of the court
festivities.

Towards the end of his life Henry was plagued with ill health – caused
primarily by his ulcerous leg and morbid obesity – and Coffer F contained
Johannes de Vigo's Latin textbook of surgery, the *Practica in arte chirurgica
compendiosa*, translated into English by Bartholomew Traheron, the royal
librarian, as *The most excellent workes of chirurgerye*. This work, which was the

first major surgical text to discuss syphilis (from which Henry did not suffer, later legends notwithstanding), was the standard medical handbook for almost a hundred years after its original publication in 1514. Henry also owned a fine medieval surgical manuscript, the *Practica chirurgia* by the twelfth-century surgeon Roger of Salerno, in a French translation. It subsequently left the royal library and is now found among the manuscripts which 'The Great Collector' and physician, Sir Hans Sloane, bequeathed to the British Museum in 1753. An expensive production, it includes many illustrations for surgical techniques as well as images of an apothecary's shop. How or why Henry obtained this codex, whose earlier provenance is unknown, or what use it would have been to him or his consultants (in spite of all the detailed drawings, it would have been difficult to work from them, since they do not necessarily relate to the text), is impossible to ascertain. (9)

In general, Henry's travelling collection appears to have been considerably less intellectual and much more eclectic than that of Francis I. This is not surprising: after the learned Hellenist Guillaume Budé had been appointed Master of the French king's library in 1522 he initiated a concerted 'acquisitions' policy, searching for manuscripts, especially Greek ones, in Italy and the Near East. Francis was himself justly proud of the collection, knew where books were stored and was concerned about their bindings. In 1536 two of his travelling chests were devoted to books and they contained works by Justinus, Thucydides, Appian and Diodorus Siculus as well as the *Destruction de Troie la grant*, the *Roman de la rose* and other romances. The contrast with the contents of Henry's chests is a telling one.

The possessions of Henry's queens (and generally speaking the goods went with the office rather than the individual) begin with a listing of the most valuable assets, the royal jewels, amongst which books with bejewelled covers could be found. Many of these were fashionable girdle-books, that is tiny devotional books, usually slightly more than two inches high and just under two inches wide, to be attached ornamentally to the waist. (10) Coffer 7 had the greatest concentration of the queen's books (sixty as well as an empty binding), arranged not by content, but by colour of binding: purple velvet garnished with silver, black velvet garnished with silver gilt, crimson velvet garnished with gold, blue velvet garnished with silver, 'murrey' velvet garnished with gold, tawny velvet garnished with silver, 'silver all over', green velvet, orange velvet, or 'covered with clothe of tissue'. Some of these books would have contained vernacular reading materials, including romances.

Most of Henry's lesser houses did not have separate library rooms and books would have been kept in the Wardrobe when not in use. Chapel books were essential in whatever residence the court found itself: like most of his wives, Henry was deeply pious and attended several religious services a day. According to the inventory begun just after his death, Ralph Tapping, sergeant of the Vestry, had in his charge sixteen graills or graduals (that is,

10. This girdle-book, even smaller than most, is bound in gold with panels and black enamel decoration. Containing the English translation of the Penitential Psalms by John Croke, one of the clerks in Chancery, it also has a tiny portrait of Henry VIII on f. 1v.
The British Library, Stowe MS 956, cover

collections of music for the Proper of the Mass), three ordinals (which set forth the order of the services), 'one booke to singe verses and graills by chil, dren', 'one booke to singe collettes on', twenty-four processionals, three mass books, one pontifical, 'two small bookes for thorganes', 'one graill for thorganes', 'ten prickesonge bookes', 'one legende for men' and one for children, 'one sermonde boke for lente'. (11)

Nowadays most people associate the monarchy with Windsor Castle, one of the lesser houses in Henry's time. During the Middle Ages Windsor was a hunting lodge, centred on the royal forest. The palace was modernized by Edward IV, and Henry VII undertook further building works, adding a new gallery and tower, the latter probably containing his private study and library. An avid sportsman, his son made good use of Windsor, especially during the earlier and more active part of his reign. According to a post-mortem inventory, the library contained in its 'nether' storey, 'borded bookes xliiii, vii pasted bookes and iii paper bookes, of which borded bookes one ys coverede with vellet and clasped with silver', and in the upper storey, 'xliiii borded bookes and ix pasted bookes'. Although none of the books is known to have survived, the description suggests that this collection consisted of older manuscripts, probably inherited from Henry VII, large printed books demanding stronger wooden bindings, supplemented by a good sprinkling of more modern and less important items in pasteboard, a recently developed binding material. The library, in other words, was being kept up to date. No doubt the grandest of the books was the one which was both bound in velvet and clasped with silver. (12) Four other jewel-encrusted books, three of which could be associated with Anne Boleyn, had already been taken off to the Jewel House in the Tower by the time the inventory was compiled.

At the greater houses hall was normally kept and this required a room large enough for the feeding of some six hundred people in several shifts, as well as accommodation for the full court. In 1526 there were six greater houses: Beaulieu, Richmond, Hampton Court, Greenwich, Eltham and Woodstock. After Wolsey's fall, Westminster was added, but three others soon fell out of favour and by the 1540s Westminster, Greenwich, Hampton

11. A processional, as its name suggests, contains the text of the litanies, hymns and prayers prescribed for use in liturgical processions. This illustration found in one of Henry's copies shows the order of the procession on Christmas Day before the Mass. The British Library, C.35.f.10, f. 8v

Court and Woodstock were the only ones remaining. It was at these four greater houses that Henry's main collections were kept.

When Henry VIII came to the throne, the principal royal library was at Richmond Palace, rebuilt by his father on the site of the old palace of Sheen after a fire in 1497; it housed the collections of Edward IV, as well as those of Henry VII. (13) We do not have a contemporary description of the library, but it would have been similar to that of Margaret of Austria (d. 1530), regent of the Netherlands. In her library there were two shelves set deskwise against the wall. The first contained fifty-two large volumes bound in velvet with gilt bosses. On the second shelf were twenty-six volumes, fifteen of which were small, bound in velvet, red satin, or cloth-of-gold, with gilt bosses. The six desks in the room had books laid out on the sloping portion to display their fine velvet bindings; other tomes, with less expensive leather bindings, were stored below. An iron trellis near the door contained twenty-seven volumes; presumably it was a shelf with an ironwork grille in front. The library also functioned as showroom for rare and beautiful objects: busts, a copy of Spinario (the Boy with a Thorn in his Foot), paintings, a square table of inlaid work, and feather dresses from 'India' presented by the Emperor.

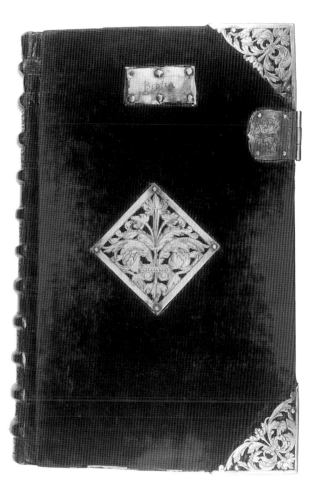

Two accounts of the library at Richmond survive from Elizabeth's reign, both made by foreign visitors. In 1600 the Czech nobleman Baron Waldstein observed: 'The next sight is Henry VII's library: it contains all kinds of books, the majority in French. Note also a chess set together with an inkstand of fine workmanship, and, beautifully set out on parchment, a genealogy of the kings of England which goes back to Adam' –

12. This Bible, which came from a monastery, was rebound for Henry VIII in a manner similar to that of the Windsor book: purple velvet with clasps and a central brass medallion.
The British Library,
Royal MS 1.D.1, cover

this latter sounding rather like something out of Gilbert and Sullivan's *The Mikado*. According to Philip Julius, duke of Stettin-Pomerania, who visited 'Ritzmund, an old house, but well built' in 1602: 'There were manuscripta highly valued by Henricus octavus; among them were many curious things, amongst others a large Bible on parchment, its letters and margin being very neatly and splendidly painted with a pen; the genealogia of the kings of England, traced to our ancestors Adam and Eve; a round mirror in which the king was said to see everything, and it was almost believed he had a spiritum familiarem sitting in it, for the mirror broke to pieces the

13. *Above* A view of Richmond
Palace from the north-east by
the Flemish artist, Anthonis van
den Wyngaerde. This drawing,
dated to 1562, was probably
executed in Spain, using sketches
Wyngaerde had made in England
whilst in the service of Phillip II
of Spain.
Society of Antiquaries, London

14. *Opposite above* Greenwich
from the river by an unknown
seventeenth-century artist. The
library wing is clearly visible.
National Trust Photographic Library

15. *Opposite below* This woodcut
illustration, taken from the
Compost et calendrier (Paris,
1499), shows the author at his
desk writing his book, a closed
book above him and others
piled up in the cupboard under
the desk.
The British Library,
L.R.41.d.2, sig. a.ii'

moment after the king's death.' (With the mirror we seem to be moving
into the world of Dr Faustus.)

No complete inventory of the Richmond library survives, but in the
Collection Moreau in the Bibliothèque nationale in Paris there is a list of
approximately one hundred and twenty-five titles from the library. Almost
all are in French and, as is typical for the period, no distinction is made
between manuscripts and printed books. This list reflects the interests of the
person, a French courtier, who compiled it, but the only hint of his identity
comes from his statement that he compiled it 'durant que je y estoye en
feuvrier 1534' (while I was there [i.e. at Richmond] in February 1534 o.s.
[= 1535 n.s.]). Towards the end of 1534 a marriage was being negotiated
between the third son of Francis I and one of the two English princesses.
Henry's relationship with Anne Boleyn was undergoing a crisis at this time
and the choice of future bride – Mary or Elizabeth – would be a telling one
for 'royal watchers'. The chief secretary to the French embassy was
Palamède Gontier, treasurer of Brittany, who visited Hampton Court in the
second half of February 1535. From Hampton Court it was just a short trip
to Richmond, where the princesses were staying, and no doubt Gontier
went there to check on their health, appearance and other vital factors.
Francis himself was, as we have seen, an ardent bibliophile and he was also
highly competitive with Henry; when at Richmond Gontier would have
been shown the library and the list he made – it must have been he – would
have fascinated his royal patron, who would no doubt have found the collection amusingly dated and rather dull, since there was virtually nothing in it
which postdated Henry VII's death. Gontier's is, however, an extremely
important document from a modern perspective, since it constitutes the first
surviving catalogue, albeit an incomplete one, of an English royal library.

To deal with the growing numbers of books which were being acquired
during the second half of his reign, Henry commanded, so his chaplain
John Leland testified, that his three principal libraries – at Greenwich, at
Hampton Court, and at Westminster – be refitted and modernized. An
ardent bibliophile, Leland considered this to be the action of a monarch of

whom one could be justly proud, and it was at these libraries that Henry's most exciting collections were formed, in part thanks to his loyal antiquary's efforts.

Henry himself was born at Greenwich and it remained one of his favourite palaces throughout his life. In 1519 important building works were undertaken and a wing projecting north fronting the Thames was added, on the second floor of which the 'highest library' was situated. (14) (As elsewhere, the library was housed at a higher level to render it safe from flooding.) No catalogue survives, but at the time of Henry's death it was furnished with seven desks, or combined lecterns and bookshelves, similar to the six in Margaret of Austria's library. (15) In the desks and under the table were three hundred and twenty-nine books, which were arranged for the most part in terms of colour: 'First in one deske xxxi bookes covered in redde; item in another deske xvi bookes covered with redde', and so forth. Some of the larger and more valuable books were described by title rather than

generically; there was, for example, 'a greate booke called an herball' and 'two greate bibles in Latten'. One of these latter is just possibly Henry's copy of the Zurich Bible of 1543: having an ornately painted fore-edge, it was bound in brown velvet, now faded and remounted, with a patterned design in gold thread, an HR monogram at the centre and Tudor roses at the edge. (16)

In Edward VI's reign books were transported from Greenwich to Westminster as part of a process of amalgamation and centralization. At this time, there was some deaccessioning and approximately thirty printed books as well as several manuscripts now at Trinity College Oxford derive from Greenwich, their earlier location – 'ex Grenewich' – noted by a mid-sixteenth-century hand in the books themselves. A number of these have been bound by the so-called Greenwich Binder – who takes his name (entirely inappropriately, in fact, since his shop was not located there), from the inscription in the books. His bindings display various royal insignia, sometimes an HR monogram, the Tudor rose, the fleur-de-lis and the portcullis. (17) Trinity College was founded in 1555 by Sir Thomas Pope, a privy councillor and an officer of the Court of Augmentations under Henry and one of the executors of his will; he seems to have obtained these books shortly after his monarch's death. As a group, they stand as a witness to the humanist component in Henry's acquisition policy: some deal with very contemporary theological issues and some are in Greek.

Until around 1525 Hampton Court was owned by Thomas Wolsey; it epitomized his cult of magnificence and was also the focus of much of the satire directed at the upwardly mobile cardinal, the mere son of an Ipswich butcher. 'Why come ye not to Court?', asked the poet and sometime royal tutor John Skelton. 'To which court? To the king's court Or to Hampton Court? Nay, to the king's court. The king's court should have the excellence but Hampton Court hath the pre-eminence.' Knowing his monarch's moods well and sensing his envy, Wolsey eventually exchanged Hampton Court for Richmond, which in turn reverted to the crown after Wolsey died in 1530. (18) Once he got possession, Henry undertook considerable building works; these occupied almost a decade and cost around £62,000, a considerable sum. Anne Boleyn was much involved in the architectural planning and a new range of lodgings were constructed for her. There was also a new tower for the housing of the library, which no

16. Queen Elizabeth's arms on the title page are a later addition to the Zurich Bible bound for her father.
The British Library, C.23.e.11, cover

doubt pleased Anne who was, as will be shown, highly literate. Apart from ex-monastic manuscripts (many of which subsequently went to Westminster), and contemporary printed books (some later acquired by Thomas Pope), the library also contained at least one tome which would be removed to the royal Jewel House by the time of Henry's death: it was an unbound copy of 'two mens translacions of the Newe Testament wrytten in vellam'. Even though there is no indication of who these two men may have been, one can assume that the translation was into English; the use of vellum indicates a book with some pretentions to grandeur.

In the second half of Henry's reign Westminster Palace (later to be known as Whitehall) replaced Greenwich as Henry's preferred residence. The old palace had been partially destroyed by fire in 1512 and was left derelict until Henry acquired York Place from Wolsey in 1529/30. York Place soon underwent major reconstruction and expansion, portions of the old Westminster Palace being incorporated into it. Anne Boleyn had originally been attracted to Westminster, as the imperial ambassador

Chapuys observed sardonically, because 'there is no lodging for the Queen [Catherine]'. As at Hampton Court, Anne showed herself keenly interested in the rebuilding, the first phase of which was completed in time for her coronation in 1533. Conveniently located next to the seat of Parliament, Westminster Palace later provided a place where Henry could reside during term time, and its administrative function was recognized by an act of Parliament in 1536, when it was officially 'demed, reputed, called and named the Kynges Paleys at Westminster for ever'. (19) As Henry got older the nature of his progresses changed and their range became narrower. He developed a more stable pattern of travel; it

17. Like other examples of work by the Greenwich Binder, Henry's copy of Sir Thomas Elyot's *The Image of Governance* has been bound in white goatskin, and has the legend REX IN AETERNVM VIVE painted on the fore-edge. In Henry's day, the fore-edge would likely have faced outward and the lettering would have been immediately visible.
The British Library, C.21.b.7, cover

18. The royal arms outside the Chapel Royal at Hampton Court; originally carved for Wolsey, they were altered and repainted for Henry VIII. Historic Royal Palaces

19. The setting for this painting is the ground floor of the king's lodgings at Westminster. The ceiling is divided into squares, each containing a royal badge.
The Royal Collection © 2004, Her Majesty Queen Elizabeth II

was centred around Westminster, where there was a resulting accretion of possessions.

Under the keepership of the privy councillor and later co-executor of Henry's will, Sir Anthony Denny (1501–49), an inventory was made in 1542 which included the detailed list of the nine hundred and ten books in the upper library. (22) The list is in two parts, reflecting the layout of the room itself. Both sections are organized in rough alphabetical sequence: in the first, printed books predominate, whereas the second is made up primarily of manuscripts from the dissolved monasteries. Each book had a number entered in it, based on an integration of the two alphabetical series: the books filed under 'A' in the first group are numbered 1 to 41; the numbering then jumps to the 'A' books in the second, which go from 42 to 84; 85 picks up the first 'B' book in the first group and so forth. (20) This is a relatively sophisti-cated system, allowing for easy retrieval of books in a society where large libraries were just coming into being. The only problem, however, is that it is closed: once books were alphabetized and numbered, newly acquired books could not be integrated into the precisely classified scheme; items had to be shifted or new sequences established, which was precisely what would hap-pen at Westminster during the amalgamations after Henry's death. (21)

Westminster was above all a working library and it was set up as such, containing 'oone table coverid with grene cloth with sondry cupbourdes in

20. *Above left* Polydore Vergil, *Prouerbiorum libellus* (Basel, 1521). The number, in this case no. 3, indicates the location of the book in the inventory. In this second edition of his adages Polydore referred very flatteringly both to Henry and to Cardinal Wolsey, who was at the height of his powers.
The British Library, 634.m.3, title page

21. *Above right* This book, *Dat boek des hyllighen Ewangelii Profecien und Epistelen* (Brunswick 1506), has been renumbered and moved twice: first it was no. 314, corresponding to the inventory entry for 'Epistolae et Euangelia in lingua germanica'; after Henry's death it was removed to a new series (no. 1359), and finally it replaced a now lost book under the heading 'Legenda sanctorum in lingua germanica' (no. 491).
The British Library, 3832.f.17, title page

22. *Right* The 1542 inventory of Westminster Palace is written in what palaeographers describe as an English bastard secretary hand with a calligraphic display script. Some of the titles on this page are specific, but others, such as 'A book of balades written', are extremely vague.
P.R.O. Misc. Books 160 (E.315/160), f. 107v

it to set bookes in with iiii olde curtens of buckeram frengid with grene silke to hang afore the bookes.' The surviving inventory reflects the evolution of Henry's ideas and policies during the course of his reign. Orthodox doctrinally, Henry saw the threats of the Lutheran heresy early on, reading and annotating with disapprobation, for example, Martin Luther's commentary on Psalm 21. His anti-Lutheran phase culminated in his *Assertio septem sacramentorum aduersus Martinum Lutherum* (published in 1521), of which six copies were to be found at Westminster, five of which were missing just after his death. Ironic, perhaps, in the light of his subsequent adventures is Henry's enthusiastic praise of the sacrament of marriage in the *Assertio*, which, so he claimed, turns 'the water of concupiscence' into 'wine of the finest flavour. Whom God hath joined together, let no man put asunder.'

Not long after this bright-eyed paean to matrimony came a sharp shift in the direction of Henry's thinking, as he began to contemplate means of putting asunder, or rather of denying altogether, his union with Catherine of Aragon. At this time the first major wave of monastic acquisitions took place, Henry's agents searching out and bringing back to their master (rather like cats with dead mice) manuscripts which might be used to challenge the pope's authority to dispense in matters which contravened divine law, such as marriage to one's brother's widow (in which case Henry's own union with his dead brother Arthur's widow was not a valid one). This campaign culminated in the tract published in the spring of 1531 outlining the opinions of the universities in England and aborad (which were for the most part favourable to Henry), the *Grauissimae atque exactissimae illustrissimarum totius Italiae et Galliae academiarum censurae.* (23) Soon afterwards Henry went even further, challenging the pope's authority in general, and the Act of Supremacy of 1534 proclaimed the imperial status of England, signalling a full break with Rome.

During this evolving anti-papal period Henry collected works, as his inventories show, by the medieval canonist and chancellor of the University of Paris, Jean Gerson, who believed that nothing necessary to salvation was to be found outside the Bible. This position had a strong resonance for Henry's advisors, as it seemingly indicated that the scriptures alone must be held up as the cornerstone of Christian belief, which greatly limited the role of the papacy, perhaps even dispensing with it altogether. As his campaign against Rome intensified, Henry turned again to monastic sources and further manuscripts began to appear in the royal libraries. At this time, Anne Boleyn being in the ascendant, reformist material in French – including translations of Luther's

23. The manuscript presentation copy of the *Censurae*, on which Henry pinned so many hopes as he attempted to rid himself of his aging Spanish queen, has been ornately bound by the King Henry's binder.
The British Library,
Harley MS 1338, cover

24. *Above* The little study also contained a 'booke of parchement conteyninge diverse paternes' which would no doubt have been similar to this design manual, bound by the Greenwich Binder with the title 'Geometria' on the cover. Divided into four sections, it contains illustrations of the five orders of architecture.

The British Library, Add. MS 34809, cover

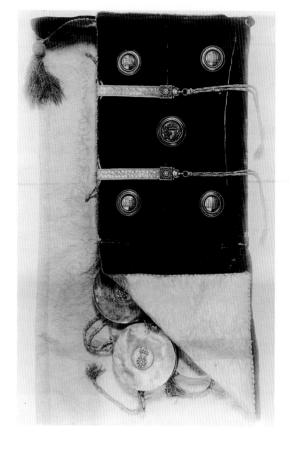

25. *Above right* In its original chemise bindings, with bosses of silver gilt enamelled and wrought with the king's arms and badges, this copy of the Foundation Indentures of Henry VII's Chapel at Westminster Abbey was removed to the Palace after the dissolution of the monastery in 1540. It was stored in the little study next to the king's old bed chamber.

The British Library,
Harley MS 1498, cover

writings – was acquired. Towards the end of the decade there was yet another shift, reflecting a movement in the direction of the German reform movement. After the failure of the Cleves marriage and the attendant fall of Cromwell in 1540, however, fewer works of religious controversy appeared in the libraries and the collection grew primarily through presentations rather than by policy as had been the case earlier in the reign.

Apart from the books in the upper library at Westminster, there were, according to a post-mortem inventory, books in the guardrobe at Westminster, the secret study, and the little study next to the king's old bed chamber. (24, 25) In the 'little study called the new library' there was a cupboard with drawers, some containing writings, including 'bokes declaring thordre of battell'. In the new library was also found 'the descripcion of the holy lande and a boke covered with vellat embrawdred with the kinges armes declaring the same in a case of blacke leather with his graces armes' – probably Wolfgang Weissenburger's *Descriptio Palestinae Nova* and its accompanying *Declaratio tabulae que descriptionem terrae sanctae continet*, published in 1538 and dedicated to Thomas Cranmer, archbishop of Canterbury, who is described as 'devoted to the teachings of Christ'. (26)

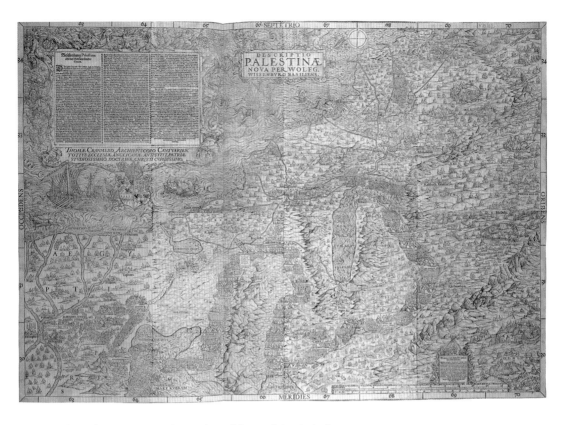

26. The focus of this map is upon the Exodus and the wandering in the desert, tents marking each encampment. Bibliothèque nationale de France, Paris

Each of the collections in the three chief houses would have been roughly similar in character, and there was constant movement from library to library. When books were brought to Henry, they were normally delivered to the palace where the court was resident, and then shifted elsewhere if required. On 26 November 1530, for example, one 'Joly Jak' was paid five shillings for bringing the king's books from Westminster to Hampton Court, and on 29 November the councillor Thomas Heneage was reimbursed for payment to a waterman transporting books from Westminster to Hampton Court. On 12 February 1531 a large shipment of books went from Greenwich to Westminster: John the king's bargeman made the journey twice in a 'grete bote' carrying 'bookes for the king'. On 18 January 1532 a bookbinder was paid for bringing books from Hampton Court to Westminster, presumably after rebinding. Sometimes matched sets – such as a twelfth-century copy of Josephus's *Antiquitates iudaicae* from St Albans (Westminster numbers 1158 + 394) – ended up in two different libraries as a result of these shifts. The movement could, in other words, be quite haphazard.

Henry must have inherited many books from his remote ancestors, but very
few of these turn up in the inventories of his palaces. One of the earliest
known to survive was stored at Richmond; it is the presentation copy to
Richard II of a verse epistle by Philippe de Mézières, ex-chancellor to King
Peter of Cyprus. Written around 1395, this poem was an eloquent plea for
an Anglo French crusade to the Holy Land, and it succeeded in its aim to
the extent that Philip of Burgundy's son John did set out for the Balkans
with a force of some ten thousand men in April 1396. Accompanying the
text is a miniature depicting the author in a grey habit offering his book to
Richard on his throne. Philippe is carrying a banner with a representation of
the Holy Lamb, symbolic of the 'Order of the Passion of Jesus Christ, conceived [by Philippe himself] forty years ago under God's inspiration, and
now to be submitted to the devotion of your Majesties.' (27)

Arthurian romances were a favourite reading matter for the upper classes
in late-medieval Europe. Written in the vernacular, these tales provided
models for chivalric behaviour and high-minded, often adulterous, passion.
The story of the doomed love of Lancelot and Guenevere was particularly
popular and many beautifully illuminated manuscripts of the prose *Lancelot
du Lac* still survive. One of these, at Richmond in 1535, is a copy written in
France in the early fourteenth century which later came into the possession of
Mary, daughter of Humphrey Bohun, earl of Hereford, Essex and North-
ampton, and later wife of Henry IV. Her arms are inserted in the initials of
the book, which is a typical way in which books, even second-hand ones,
were personalized by their owners. (28) A series of miniatures accompanies
the text, including one with a paired sequence of events rather like the
frames in a modern cartoon. (29)

Mary Bohun was the mother of Henry V, who owned a number of
books, including Geoffrey Chaucer's *Troilus and Criseyde*. He also had a history in Latin excerpted from the chronicle of the English monk at St
Evrault in Normany, Orderic Vitalis (1075–c.1143), describing the death
and final bequests of Henry's noble ancestor William the Conqueror.
Henry captured Caen in 1415 and the monks presented him with this manuscript after the signing of the 1420 Treaty of Troyes which reinstated
English rule in Normandy. The excerpted sections of Orderic are organized
to form a subtle appeal by the monks for restitution of their English estates.
In a general sense, then, this manuscript fits into the 'mirror for princes'
genre, of which the Alliterative *Morte Arthure* is a vernacular example.
Through historical models of both the good and the bad, the ruler is
instructed in the ways to be a responsible and generous prince.

Henry V's younger brother, Humfrey, duke of Gloucester, donated two
hundred and seventy-nine manuscripts to the University of Oxford between
1439 and 1444 and these were housed in a specially built room over the

present Divinity Schools. Not everything went to Oxford, however, and four of his books appear in the Henrician inventories. One is a copy of *Le songe du vergier* ('Dream of the Woodsman'), first written in Latin for the French king Charles V in 1376, but translated into French two years later. In the manner of Chaucer's early works, the poem is cast as a dream vision and consists of a dialogue between a clerk and a knight concerning secular and ecclesiastical power, specifically the power of the papacy, a topic which would later be of great concern to Duke Humfrey's Tudor descendant. (31) Humfrey acquired this book from his brother, John, duke of Bedford, who purchased it from the Louvre library in 1425. Humfrey also owned a deluxe copy, containing more than four hundred miniatures, of the *Grandes chroniques de France*, first composed at the abbey of St Denis at the end of the fourteenth century and then elaborated further: in its fullest form it provided a history of the kings of France from their putative Trojan origins up to 1461. (30) When it was stored at Richmond this manuscript was bound in red velvet: the seventeenth-century antiquary and collector Sir Robert Cotton would describe it as having 'fair pictures of the old form, the best book'.

Saints' Lives were a ubiquitous part of the literary culture of the Middle Ages and in the retraction to his *Canterbury Tales* Chaucer lamented that he had not devoted more of his energies to their composition. After the twelve-year-old King Henry VI paid a prolonged visit to the Benedictine Abbey of Bury St Edmunds in December 1433, the abbot requested the poet John Lydgate to compose lives of Saints Edmund and Fremund in commemoration of the occasion (and of the saint to whom the monastery was dedicated). The resulting poem includes a description of the young king's visit to the martyr's shrine, and this was illustrated in the presentation manuscript. (33) The later history of this glorious production is difficult to trace, although it was certainly at Westminster Palace in 1542. It contains the signature of John Touchet, eighth baron Audley (d. 1559); it must therefore have left royal hands at some point in the fifteenth century to have been acquired by Audley, who then presented it to Henry VIII in gratitude for his restoration in blood and honours in 1512. Audley also gave Henry a copy of Lydgate's Troy book: Henry, who was campaigning against France, was intrigued by the Troy story, and he commissioned Richard Pynson, the King's Printer, to publish Lydgate's text as a stimulus to military endeavour. He was, no doubt, pleased with both of Audley's gifts: the latter for its topicality, the former because of the devotion of his grandmother, Lady Margaret Beaufort, to the saintly Henry VI.

Although a number of books with Richard III's signature survive – he had a rich and varied collection – only one of these appears in the catalogues of Henry's libraries, a manuscript of the *Grandes chroniques de France*. Like the copy owned by Humfrey, it was stored at Richmond. (34) It is likely that Richard's copy of Guido delle Colonne's *Historia destructionis Troiae* ('History of the Destruction of Troy'), composed in 1278, remained in the royal library until the mid-seventeenth century: it has been signed by James I and Charles I. Later it was abstracted by Oliver Cromwell, whose signature, dated 1656, is found on fol. 1, just above that of 'Ricardus Rex'. Ultimately

27. *Right* A man stands behind the author with a mace; to the right of Richard are four courtiers, three of whom sport the very long shoes affected in the period and much censured by contemporary preachers.
The British Library,
Royal MS 20. B.vi, f. 2

28. *Above* Mary Bohun's arms are prominent: England (gules, 3 lions passant gardant or) and Bohun (azure, a bend argent cotised or, between 6 lions of the last).
The British Library,
Royal MS 20. D.iv, f. 1.

29. *Right* In the first scene we see an encapsulation of the tragedy which will bring about the fall of the whole Round Table. Arthur, the dutiful king and leader of the nation, is engaged in conversation with his barons whilst Lancelot, smitten by love, is whispering to Guenevere. In the second scene, king and queen have both assumed their public role and preside over a state banquet.
The British Library,
Royal MS 20. D.iv, f. 1.

Quatre cens et quatre
ans auant que la ci
te de Rome fust fondee
regnoit Priauz en
Troie la grant. il en
uoia Paris la mere
de ses filz en Grece pour rauir eleine la

des princes de la cite qui sespandirent
en diuerses parties du monde pour quer
re nouueles habitaations. Comme Ixle
nius. eneas. et enderno2. et maint au
tre. Cil Ixlenius fu li vns des filz au roy
priant. si ert poetes et bons clers. cil et
CC. emmena auecques li des essillies de

30. *Above* Like the British, the
French traced their origin to the
Trojans and one of the illustrations
in this manuscript of the *Grandes
chroniques* gives a thumbnail sketch
of the Trojan war: (i) Priam sends
Paris on a diplomatic mission to
Sparta where he will meet Helen,
wife of King Menelaus; (ii) Paris
elopes with Helen and travels to
Asia; (iii) this inevitably leads
to the siege and fall of Troy.
The British Library,
Royal MS 16.G.VI, f. 4v

31. *Left* The first miniature lays
out the theme of *Le songe du vergier*,
showing Charles enthroned between
two queens who represent spiritual
and temporal power. In front of him
are the clerk and the knight; in the
foreground the dreamer lies on
the ground.
The British Library,
Royal MS 19.C.IV, f. 1v

this copy found its way into the collection of Peter Dubrovsky, who rescued many books at the time of the French revolution, and it is now in St Petersburg, as is Richard's copy of Geoffrey of Monmouth's *Historia regum Britanniae* ('History of the Kings of Britain').

Individually impressive though they might be, this group of inherited books does not add up to a great deal, and the real founder of the royal library – in terms of manuscripts, at least – was Richard III's oldest brother Edward IV. During the brief restoration of Henry VI in 1470–71, Edward IV was exiled to Burgundy and lodged with Louis de Gruuthuse, governor of Holland and Zeeland, whose library he greatly admired and wished to emulate. Soon after his restoration he assembled his own collection and he did so over an extremely brief period, as is made abundantly clear by the staggeringly large bill of £240 by one Philip Maisertuell for books bought abroad in 1479. This was a period of affluence for Edward and the collection is a direct result of a brief lull during the Wars of the Roses.

Twenty-one illuminated manuscripts carrying Edward's arms and devices derive from the Burgundian Netherlands. A further twenty-eight manuscripts can be linked to him on grounds of heraldry, illumination, or script. No doubt, part of the purpose of this group was to educate Edward's ill-fated sons, the Princes in the Tower, and approximately half a dozen manuscripts have armorial bearings of Edward V and Richard, duke of York. (35) These books are all in French translation or by French authors and provide instruction in history (the *Speculum historiale*), princely behaviour (Alain Chartier's *Le breviaire des nobles*), classical history (Valerius Maximus's *Memorabilia, Les faits des romains*), and theology (St Augustine's *De ciuitate Dei*, Peter Comestor's *Historia scholastica*). All are richly illuminated – learning was to be conveyed through delight – and extremely bulky, no doubt meant to be read on a lectern. These were not, however, the heaviest of Edward's books – it was a large collection in every way – and the most substantial item weighed in at just under forty pounds. This is the French translation of Boccaccio's *De casibus illustrium uirorum et feminarum* ('On the Fall of Illustrious Men and Women') by Laurent de Premierfait, made for Jean, duc de Berry, himself now remembered primarily for his *Très riches heures*. (42) Boccaccio's stories were exemplary, showing how even the wealthiest and most powerful in this sublunar world are governed by fortune's wheel, doomed by an implacable fate. (32) As Chaucer's monk made droningly clear, this inevitable fall – not Aristotle's hubris or Shakespeare's character flaw – provided the definition of tragedy during the Middle Ages:

> Tragedy means a certain kind of story,
> As old books tell, of those who fell from glory,
> People that stood in great prosperity
> And were cast down out of their high degree
> Into calamity, and so they died.

The first printed book in England was issued in Edward's reign; it was William Caxton's edition in 1477 of an English rendering by Edward's brother-in-law, Anthony Wydville, of a French translation of the popular medieval compendium of *Dicta philosophorum*. Wydville did not present the king with a printed copy of his version, entitled *The Dictes or Sayengis of the Philosophres*, but had a manuscript specially prepared. (38) This practice of producing separate manuscript copies to accompany printed editions – often, as in this case, differing significantly one from the other – would carry on into Henry VIII's reign, when Erasmus, for example, presented the young king with a manuscript copy of his translation from Greek into Latin of Plutarch's *De discrimine adulatoris et amici* ('How to tell a flatterer from a friend'), which is now found in Cambridge University Library as Additional Manuscript 6858.

Covers by nature are particularly vulnerable to damage and decay: none of the original bindings of Edward IV's books is still intact, but there is a bill from 1480 – almost £12 not including the cost of the velvet – for the 'binding, gilding and dressing of the books'. The actual structure consisted of wooden boards covered with velvet – six yards of crimson figured velvet were needed for this group of books. The clasps were gilt and would no doubt have been highly ornamented; so too perhaps the bosses which would have been attached to the front cover in a quincunx pattern. At the time when Sir Robert Cotton was examining the Richmond library in the early seventeenth century, the books were still in their original covers and he describes bindings of three of the six books he was after: two were bound in blue velvet and one in red; in one case the cover was 'broken'.

Edward's books were probably stored at his palace at Eltham in Middlesex, where extensive renovations, including substantial repairs to the library, were undertaken between 1477 and 1485. When Henry VII ascended the throne in 1485 the Yorkist goods and chattels, including palaces and books, passed to him. Like Edward, Henry enjoyed sumptuous manuscripts and in at least one case he was responsible for the completion of a book begun for his predecessor, a copy of the highly popular poems of Charles d'Orléans, the French prince and father of Louis XII, who spent many years in exile in England after Henry V's victory at Agincourt. (40) According to the French ambassador, Claude de Seyssel, Henry VII took great delight in reading, or rather in hearing books read – during the Tudor reign, as earlier, important personages preferred to have somebody else to do the menial work of actually deciphering the letters. Henry favoured histories and other works suitable to the edification of a noble and wise prince; not unexpectedly, therefore, Seyssel presented the king with his own translation into French of the *Anabasis* of the Greek historian, Xenophon, pupil of Socrates.

Seyssel undertook this translation towards the end of Henry VII's reign and he was highly flattering about the royal library at Richmond, to which Edward's books had been moved, describing it as very beautiful and wonderfully outfitted. As early as 1492 the king had appointed a Fleming, Quentin Poulet of Lille, to be royal librarian – and this is the first time such a title was used in England. Poulet was also a scribe and he was responsible for copying *L'Imagination de la vraie noblesse* – a French adaptation of Ramón Lull's discussion of nobility in the form of Imagination's discourse to a knight – completed at Sheen on the last day of June 1496 (the palace was

32. *Above left* Zenobia, queen of Palmyra, was seen as a representative tragic heroine and her public exhibition at Aurelian's triumph in Rome is one of the many events illustrated in this copy of *De casibus*.
The British Library,
Royal MS 14.E.v, f. 406v

33. *Above right* Surrounded by his courtiers and religious attendants, Henry VI kneels at the tomb of the murdered St Edmund.
The British Library,
Harley MS 2278, f. 4v

34. *Right* Richard III's signature in the form 'Richard Gloucestre', is found towards the bottom of the left column of the *Grandes chroniques*; at the top of the right there is an illuminated initial showing the siege of Meaux and the death of the mayor.
The British Library,
Royal MS 20.C.VII, f. 134r

35. *Opposite* This miniature from the French translation of Vincent of Beauvais's compendium of history, the *Speculum historiale*, shows Vincent at his desk. In the border Edward IV's arms appear three times, once in a shield encircled by the Garter, with the arms of his sons in shields flanking it.
The British Library,
Royal MS 14.E.I, f. 3r

De la cause de seuure emprinse.
Premier chapitre.

Our ce que la multi-
tude des liures, et la
brieuete du temps et
la foibleffe du mém-
ne seuffrent pas les
chofes qui sont efcriptes eftre com-
prinses enfemble en vnf couraige
ce meft aduis a moy qui suis le

momdre de tous mes freres en facce.
Et ce puis ie fcauoir en moy mefmes
qui ay veu feu et retourne plufieurs
siures y moult long temps affidueile-
ment et auitreufement. Et neatmois
par le confeil dauifaue de mes pl' fou-
uerains et crreigneurs auffaues fle-
que iay efleues y mon prtit engin
A bien feu de tous fes fiures de mê
foy catholique ou des fiures pasens

destroyed by fire the following year). (39) In the same year the Italian poet Johannes Michael Nagonius visited England and presented Henry with a volume of Latin poetry in which Henry was portrayed as an epic hero whose most impressive deeds were yet to come. Based on the imagery of Petrarch's highly popular *Trionfi*, the frontispiece shows Henry riding in a triumphal car drawn by two white horses. (36) The manuscript pleased the king mightily and he wrote to this effect to Cardinal Francesco Todeschini-Piccolomini, the future Pope Pius III, who had sent letters of recommendation with Nagonius. As was so often the case, a book thus occupied a complex role in a system of exchange of favours. Another Italian writer, Johannes Opicius, presented Henry with five short poems in Latin: these were conceived as hymns to 'the sacred majesty of the magnanimous king of the British'; they commemorated his valorous deeds and celebrated the union of the white and red rose. (The celebration of the Tudor rose would become a commonplace in poetry and visual art, especially after the accession of Henry's son, who combined both bloodlines in his veins; or as John Skelton put it, 'The rose both white and red / In one rose now doth grow'.) Opicius made it abundantly clear that in return for his tributes he hoped Henry would 'lend aid [to] a foundering' and provide him with financial support. (41) Benedictus Opicius, probably Johannes's brother, was one of the composers whose music featured in an illuminated musical manuscript which his father, Petrus, had made for the king in 1516.

Henry VII inherited books, including two from his sister-in-law Cecily, third daughter of Edward IV, who had received them from the family of her relatively humble husband John, Viscount Welles. One, transcribed perhaps in Flanders in the late thirteenth century, consists of translations into French of civil law texts by Justinian. (Justinian's great sixth-century compilation, the *Corpus iuris ciuilis*, was the cornerstone of the medieval legal stystem throughout Europe.) The other was also written in the thirteenth century and contains both the popular manual of penitence written for the laity by Pierre d'Abernon of Fetcham, entitled *La Lumere as lais*, and a glossed French prose version of the Apocalypse. Bound into it is a flyleaf which gives a list of fourteen titles of books, presumably belonging to the Welles family, including a copy of *The Canterbury Tales* and 'a boke cald mort Arthro'. (37)

Towards the end of the fifteenth century the printing press was revolutionizing the book trade and Henry VII seems to have had some sort of

36. Carrying his sceptre and orb and wearing an imperial crown Henry VII sits on a throne composed from classical volutes and a scallop shell niche. This is one of several Henrician books which later migrated to York Minster.
Copyright © Dean and Chapter of York: by kind permission, MS XVI.N.2, f. 5v

37. Henry also owned a copy of the revised Wycliffite translation into English of the Bible (dating to the early fifteenth century), which has been personalized by the addition of a border with the Tudor rose, daisy and portcullis as well as the royal arms.
The British Library,
Royal MS I.C.VIII, f. Ir

'standing order' with the prominent Parisian publisher and book‑seller Antoine Vérard, who published religious, chivalric, classical and historical texts at the request of the French royal family and nobility. Vérard produced deluxe books in large and expensive folio format; printed on vellum as well as paper with woodcuts which were then overpainted by manuscript painters, these were often personalized for important owners such as Charles VIII of France, his consort Anne de Bretagne, Louise de Savoie, her son Francis I, and Henry VII himself. Among Henry's purchases from Vérard, six have the English royal arms added, and others show signs of having been adapted for Henry's use even though the arms have been left blank. (46). In subsequent generations Henry's printed books came to be viewed as less valuable commodities than the manuscripts, and they were

38. This added presentation miniature shows Wydville and another figure, perhaps his scribe, offering the book to Edward IV, his wife and heirs.

Lambeth Palace Library, MS 265, frontispiece, f. vi^v

39. The miniatures in Poulet's manuscript are in the Flemish style; in the first a crowned Henry VII receives the book from the writer.

The British Library, Royal MS 19.C.VIII, f. 1

40. The Tower of London with London Bridge behind is illustrated here. Chronology ignored, the exiled Charles d'Orléans is seen simultaneously writing at a window, and in the court sending the letter. The arms of Henry VII, supported by lions, are found in the border.

The British Library, Royal MS 16.F.II, f. 73

41. The first initial of 'De regis laudibus sub praetextu rosae purpureae' shows the Beaufort portcullis. The rustic shepherds at the bottom of the page provide a visual indication that the poem is to be a pastoral verse dialogue.

The British Library, Cotton MS Vespasian B.IV, f. 14r

42. The first of the seventy-six miniatures in this copy of the *De casibus* shows the duc de Berry receiving the book from his translator. He is surrounded by courtiers, a jester, and a dwarf with his performing dog and his ape. In the background there is a carved chimney piece and a settle.

The British Library, Royal MS 14.E.v, f. 5

thus more vulnerable to deaccession: for example, his copy on vellum of Guillaume de Deguilleville's *Le pelerinage de vie humaine*, a thirteenth-century allegorical poem of a sort which was greatly popular in the declining Middle Ages, is now, after having travelled extensively, at the Huntington Library in San Marino, California. The book can be identified as Henry's by the border design which features the Tudor insignia, the red rose of Lancaster, the Beaufort portcullis; the arms are those of England supported by the red dragon and white greyhound of Henry's dynasty. (43)

Scholars still debate Henry VII's attraction to printed books: was it part and parcel of his legendary parsimony, did it show a lack of discrimination

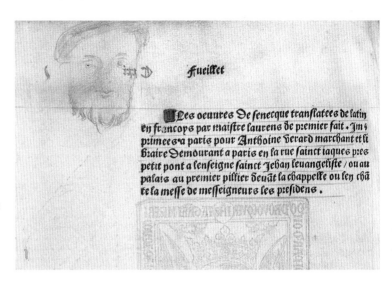

43. What is almost certainly the royal copy on vellum of the Vérard edition of the French translation of the works of Seneca is now at Trinity College Cambridge. For some reason a Holbeinesque sketch of Henry VIII has been inserted somewhat later, perhaps to indicate the book's earlier provenance.

The Master and Fellows of Trinity College, Cambridge, VI.18.82, back flyleaf

or was it because he was excited to be at the cutting edge of a new technology? Are they 'treasures' or are they, as Arundell Esdaile put it in his history of the British Museum Library (1946), 'merely cheap imitations of French illuminated manuscripts, with woodcuts smothered in coarse colour, such as an economical king like Henry VII would naturally prefer'? What can be said for certain is that although Henry's Vérards were generally not as expensive and elaborately embellished as those of his French counterparts, they were not at the bottom end of the market either and he paid, for example, a goodly £6 for a copy of *Le jardin de santé*. He seems to have owned two copies of this particular work, a translation of the *Ortus sanitatis* – one of the earliest printed herbals in Europe (in which the dandelion is first mentioned and the narcissus is portrayed sporting a human head). The copy on paper is still in the British Library, but that on vellum containing a hand-painted woodcut of the presentation of the book to Henry VII, his arms and supporters in the lower border, has long since migrated and is now found in an altogether unexpected location: the Clara S. Peck Collection of the Transylvania University Special College in Lexington, Kentucky.

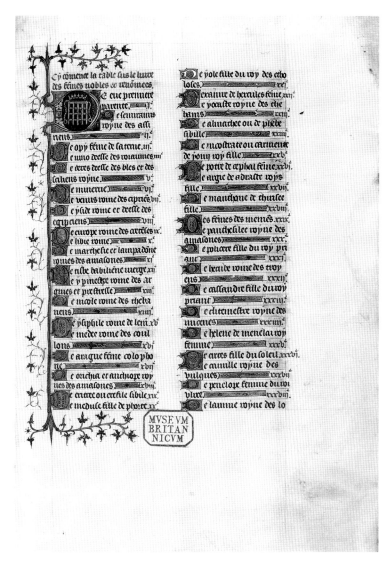

44. *Left* Although this copy of *De claris mulieribus* was written in the early fifteenth century, the Beaufort badge, a portcullis and chains surmounted by a coronet, have later been introduced into this initial.
The British Library,
Royal MS 20.C.v, f. 1

45. *Below* This posthumous portrait by Rowland Lockey (*c.*1598) shows Lady Margaret surrounded by her formal and informal iconography: the Beaufort portcullis appears behind her in the cloth-of-gold and in the window; the Beaufort arms are surmounted by a coronet with a swan and yale as supporters. The book in front attests to her rich devotional life.
By permission of the Master and Fellows of St John's College, Cambridge

Henry VII's mother, Lady Margaret Beaufort, was renowned for her patronage of scholars and she was also a translator in her own right. (45) It is just possible that the copy of the French translation of Boccaccio's *De claris mulieribus* ('On Famous Womeμn') which was at Westminster in 1542 belonged to her and is to be identified as the 'greatte volume of velom named John Bokas lymned [illuminated]' which she left to her younger grandson. (44) Cicero was especially admired by humanist educators and one of the treasures of the library at Emmanuel College Cambridge is a copy of the *editio princeps* of Cicero's *De officiis*, printed on vellum at Mainz in 1465. (47) This book was a gift to Prince Arthur by his grandmother, Lady Margaret obviously well aware that visual delight helps whet the appetite for learning. Another book, the second volume of Jean Froissart's chronicles of the

Le prologue

Pres que sounet & bien / longuemēt ap eu pour / pēse en moymesmes le / dit et auctoute de aristo / te qui dit au commence / ment de sa methaphisique. Omnes / hoīes natura scire desiderāt. Qui est / adire que tout hōme naturellemēt desi / re scauoir selon ce que en mon petit & de / bile entendemēt ap peu cōsiderer & cōt

46. This copy of the French translation of Vincent of Beauvais's *Speculum historiale* has been rebound in red velvet in five volumes. The woodcut depicting a presentation to a king has been painted over to represent Henry, but there is a blank space where one might have expected the king's arms. The British Library, C.22.d.1, sig. A1v

3.3.45

47. Illuminations have been inserted in the printed copy of *De officiis*: Tudor badges, the Prince of Wales's feathers and a historiated initial portraying Prince Arthur and his seated teacher. The artist responsible for these illuminations is known as the Master of the Dark Eyes and his chief patron was Lady Margaret. Reproduced by permission of the Master and Fellows of Emmanuel College, MS 5.3.11, f. 1

Hundred Years War, has the Prince of Wales's feathers inserted and may also have belonged to Arthur. (48) Certainly Lady Margaret owned at least one copy of the second volume of Froissart; it is mentioned in her will, where it was left to Henry VIII. It has not been possible to identify the copy of John Lydgate's *Siege of Troy*, nor the 'French book', prefaced with an illuminated version of Genesis, which Lady Margaret also bequeathed Henry when she died – supposedly from a surfeit of swan – in 1509.

48. The surviving first initial is decorated with the arms of England; the crest, cap of maintenance and helmet are still visible. The feathers of the Prince of Wales have been added in all the borders.
The British Library,
Arundel MS 67, vol. 2, f. 1r

NEW YEAR'S GIFTS,

OTHER PRESENTATIONS AND PURCHASES

On 3 January 1538 – in spite of his healthy new son this was not a happy season for the recently widowed Henry – John Husee wrote to his master Arthur Plantagenet, Viscount Lisle, describing New Year's Day at Court:

> The King stood leaning against the cupboard, receiving all things; and Mr. [Sir Brian] Tuke at the end of the same cupboard, penning all things that were presented; and behind his Grace stood Mr. Kingston and Sir John Russell, and beside his Grace stood the Earl of Hertford and my Lord Privy Seal. There was but a small Court.

Husee proudly recorded that the Lord Privy Seal (the ever vigilant Thomas Cromwell), singled him out for the notice of the king who, in turn, made gracious comments to him: 'It was gently done of my Lord Privy Seal', as Husee complacently observed, 'to have your lordship in remembrance, setting the matter so well forward.' The scene recreates vividly both the ritual of the New Year's Day gift-giving ceremony and the potential for favour which lay behind it. The nobility and clergy were all expected to exchange gifts with the monarch and there was a strict hierarchy; the ultimate aim was to have one's contribution admired in order that one's interests ('the matter') might be forwarded in the following months. Many of the 'modern' books in Henry's collection derive from this annual ceremony. As the surviving Henrician gift-rolls indicate, most came from individuals who had literary connections: court poets such as Bernard André, printers such as Thomas Berthelet, and professional bookmen such as John Leland, who on New Year's Day 1539 provided the aging king both with 'a booke furnisshed with silver and gilte' and a 'lokeing glasse to lay uppon [it]'. Among the gifts that still survive, one finds a mixture of manuscripts and printed books, some of the latter on vellum and personalized in a variety of ways, some paper copies with tipped-in dedications. When Leland, for example, gave the king a copy of the 1528 edition of the commentaries on Paul's Epistles by the ninth-century scholar Sedulius Scotus, he inserted verses of his own composing which concluded with the hope that 'you will receive this gift with a cheerful face, a token of my feelings towards you'. Some books came from supplicants seeking patronage, others from people fearing disfavour. Certain of the individuals offering their own compositions had been associated with the court for years before Henry's birth and several had occupied positions as tutors to Henry and his older brother Arthur.

Manuscripts

A significant number of the artists and writers attached to the royal household had emigrated from abroad, primarily Italy and France. One of the chief of these, the continental poet Pietro Carmeliano of Brescia (1451–1528), had a long and productive association with the English court. He first set out to capture royal notice through his Latin poem *De uere* ('On Spring') executed for the young Edward, Prince of Wales, at Easter 1482. As he proclaimed quite openly in the preface: 'I thought for a

49. *Left* Appropriately, the opening stanzas of Carmeliano's verses on spring have an illuminated border which incorporates a flower motif of English design.
The British Library,
Royal MS 12.A.XXIX, f. 1r

50. *Right* The royal arms, crowned, supported by the dragon and white greyhound, are depicted. During the first part of the reign Henry's supporters were a dragon dexter and a greyhound sinister. Around 1528 the greyhound was dropped, the dragon moved to the sinister side and the lion was introduced.
By courtesy of The Marquess of Salisbury,
Cecil Papers, MS 277/1, f. 1r

long time, illustrious prince, about how I might make myself known to your highness and finally I decided that it might be possible if I were to give you some of my verses'. (49) Carmeliano presented the prince's father, Edward IV, with a printed copy of Cicero's *Orator* (Venice, 1478), prefaced by his own compositions; Richard III received a manuscript copy of his life of St Catherine of Alexandria. After Henry VII overthrew Richard, Carmeliano prudently switched allegiance and wrote encomia on Henry's marriage to Elizabeth of York and shortly afterwards on the birth of Arthur, for whom he would act as tutor. In the 'joyful exhortation' on the young prince's birth, he distanced himself as thoroughly as possible from his former Yorkist patrons, denouncing Richard as a criminal tyrant, capable of any evil imaginable. In 1498 Carmeliano was made Latin secretary to the king and continued in this office into the reign of Henry VIII. Like many other foreign courtiers he also acted as an intelligence agent and regularly sent information on English activities to the Venetians.

Born in Toulouse around 1450 and trained in law, the blind poet and Austin friar Bernard André came to England at the close of the Wars of the Roses and his earliest surviving work is a paean to Henry VII's triumphant entry into London in 1485. Soon afterwards he was paid a regular salary as the king's 'poeta laureatus', although there is no evidence that he (or any other

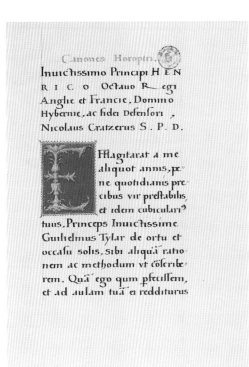

Tudor poet) was actually crowned with laurel in the Petrarchan manner. He continued in the service of Henry's second son until his own death around 1522, although, as in the case of Carmeliano, his influence temporarily decreased when Henry VIII first came to the throne and put his own people in place. Apart from writing epideictic verse and propaganda for state occasions, André presented New Year's gifts; ten survive, six of which were gifts to Henry VIII. In the earliest of these, his 'Exposition du Pseaulme huitiesme', he provided a tribute to Henry and his first queen; he also employed a device much beloved by contemporary poets abroad by organizing the lines into an acrostic giving the names and titles of Henry and Catherine. The presentation copy of André's encomiastic verses on Henry's victory over the French and Scots in 1513 is now at Hatfield House: it is one of a number of royal books that went to Hatfield during Elizabeth's reign, presumably as gifts to William Cecil, first baron Burghley, Elizabeth's secretary and lord treasurer. (50)

Pieter Meghen (1466/7–1540), the one-eyed, hard-drinking Flemish scribe, appropriately dubbed 'Cyclops' by Erasmus, was long resident in

51. *Left* This initial was executed by Hans Holbein the Younger. A duplicate version of the text – which explained the use of the 'horoptrum' (an instrument which could determine the time of sunrise and sunset and had other functions) – was probably meant for presentation to Henry on New Year's Day 1538.
Bodleian Library, Oxford,
Bodley MS 504. Initial E on f. 1r

52. *Right* Maillart, seated at his desk, is shown wearing royal livery with the HR monogram on his tunic. His eyes are lifted up to God in Heaven and he prays that his new work will be 'agreable' to the king.
Bodleian Library, Oxford,
Bodley MS 883, f. 1v

England and was closely associated with the learned humanist John Colet, founder of St Paul's School, for whom he executed several beautiful manu-scripts of biblical texts, including a Latin translation of the Pauline Epistles by the French reformer Jacques Lefèvre d'Etaples. Between 1511 and 1519 he often acted as courier to friends and patrons and conveyed to Henry a presentation copy of Erasmus's *Institutio principis Christiani* ('Institution of a Christian Prince') and of Plutarch's works (both published at Basel in 1516), now at Charlecote Park, Warwickshire. Bound into the volume is a vellum leaf containing the royal arms, encircled by the Garter and sur-mounted by a crown, supported by the red dragon and white greyhound. Meghen's own finest efforts went to Henry, as one would expect, and in 1528/9 he executed a copy of a short astronomical treatise, *Canones horoptri*, by Nicholas Kratzer, the King's Astronomer (as well as 'deviser of the king's horologes'), and dedicated by the author to the king. (51) Meghen was suitably rewarded for his endeavours and occupied a position as Writer of the King's Books from 1530 until his death some ten years later.

Jean Maillart, an accomplished poet and painter from Rouen, came to England from the court of Francis I in 1539 and received payments as royal orator in the French tongue until 1541; doubtless his ambition was to become an official poet in the manner of Clément Marot in France. Four of his presentations to Henry still survive: two were brought to Westmin-ster soon after Henry's death and two were retained at other palaces. Two, moreover, still have their original red velvet binding, one with silver gilt corner pieces and remains of clasps. One eventually left the royal collec-tion and is now found in the Bodleian Library at Oxford. (52) Called *Le chemin du paradis* ('The Path to Paradise') and composed shortly before 1540, it consists of an abridgement of the principal Christian doctrines, meant to function as an aid to the faithful in their quest for salvation. Henry, to whom the poem is dedicated and whose arms are displayed at the beginning of the prefatory epistle, is described as king of England and France; he is praised both for his piety and for his stand against heresy, a 'true defender of the faith'. As Maillart explains, the poem was first shown to a certain bishop to make sure of its orthodoxy and in fact it occupies an intermediary position between Luther and the Roman church in terms of doctrine. Maillart's most sumptuous piece of work is an illu-minated psalter in Latin, which is signed 'Johannes Mallardus, regius ora-tor, et ex calamo regi Anglie et Francie fidei defensori invictissimo' (Jean Maillart, royal orator: from his pen to the most invincible king of England and France, and defender of the faith). Henry was much taken with it and the manuscript contains a number of his marginalia, in some of which he notes the parallels between his situation and that of his fabled biblical predecessor, King David. (53) What is relatively unusual about Maillart's work is that he was often the scribe and illuminator as well as the author; in one manuscript he describes himself grandly as 'escripvain, cosmo-graphe et mathematicien'.

Maps and exploration fascinated Henry, who was born just one year before Christopher Columbus discovered America, and around 1540

Maillart presented him with 'Le premier livre de la cosmographie', a poetic rendering of *Les Voyages avantureux* of Jean Alfonse de Santonge, a French naviagator engaged in a search for the North-west Passage. Like many other itinerant writers Maillart was adept at recycling material and Francis had already received a version entitled 'Premier livre de la description de tous les ports de mer de l'univers'. The work was, as Maillart explained, a description of both places and peoples – the Germans, for example, characterized as excessive drinkers of beer and wine – and more practically, there are useful discussions of winds and navigation. (54)

The most sophisticated of Henry's cartographic books were prepared by Jean Rotz, a French mariner of Scottish descent, who arrived in England in 1542 and almost immediately established himself as the first Hydrographer Royal. Rotz was an experienced mariner and had travelled widely; information from his own voyages, including to Guinea and Brazil, was incorporated into his charts. Soon after he settled in England he composed a treatise 'on the variation of the magnetic compass and of certain notable facts hitherto unknown concerning the errors in navigation', which was meant 'for the use and recreation of those who liked to taste the fruit of astrology and marine science'. (55) Also prepared in 1542 was his 'Boke of Idrography', which had originally been intended for Francis, but which was adapted for Henry. In the preface Rotz proclaimed that the book dealt with all hydrography (i.e. the study of seas, lakes, rivers and other waters) and marine science. It was a lavish production, the borders embellished with designs harking back to Ghent–Bruges models; many of the charts contained the results of Rotz's first-hand observation. (56)

As the efforts of the pioneering Tudor sonneters Sir Thomas Wyatt and Henry Howard, earl of Surrey, forcefully remind us, translation was considered an essential courtly accomplishment in the Tudor period. Generally speaking, these effusions (both poetry and longer prose texts from the classical world) were meant for an exclusive and closed audience of courtly readers, Henry and his intimates, and they were never intended to be put into print, a medium which still had a stigma about it. (In this area, as in many others, Henry was less progressive than Francis, who began a conscious practice in the 1520s of making translations of the ancient historians available in print.) It was also assumed that the readers of many of the poetic translations would be closely familiar with the original text. The point of the exercise, then, was to show off one's verbal finesse, often through the use of rhetorical figures and aureate diction. Subtle differences from the originals, moreover, often encapsulated hidden meanings.

Apart from the spectacular efforts by these courtly makers, his own brother-in-law George Boleyn included, Henry also had a good selection of more workaday translations, such as the conservative theologian John Harpsfield's rendering into Latin of the commentary on the first book of Aristotle's Physics by the Greek philosopher Simplicius of Cilicia; the royal tutor Sir John Cheke's Latin version of Maximus the Confessor's *Liber asceticus*; the German reformer Georg Burckhardt's translation into Latin as *De purgatorio* of Martin Luther's *Eyn Widerruff vom Fegefeür*.

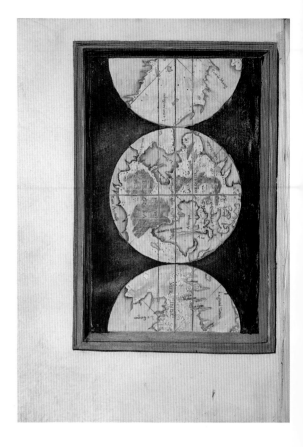

53. *Above left and detail below* To Henry's right in this illumination is his jester, William Sommer, who is introduced into the scene by way of an ironic allusion to the accompanying Psalm (Vulg. Ps. 52:1): 'The fool says in his heart, "There is no God".'
The British Library, Royal MS 2.A.XVI, f. 63v

54. *Above right* Although only the first volume of Maillart's projected topographical work – covering Spain, France, Britain, North Germany and carrying on down the coast of America to the Straits of Magellan – was completed, it does contain a coloured map of the whole world in hemispheres.
The British Library, Royal MS 20.B.XII, f. 5

55. *Above opposite* Rotz's differential quadrant, illustrated here, combined a magnetic compass and universal dial, and was meant to deal with the navigational problems of contemporary charts.
The British Library, Royal MS 20.B.VII, f. 1v–2r

56. *Below opposite* The figures on the bar scale of this chart of America and the Pacific Ocean may represent Rotz and a colleague; Rotz also appears on a star map elsewhere in the manuscript.
The British Library, Royal MS 20.E.IX, f. 7v–8r

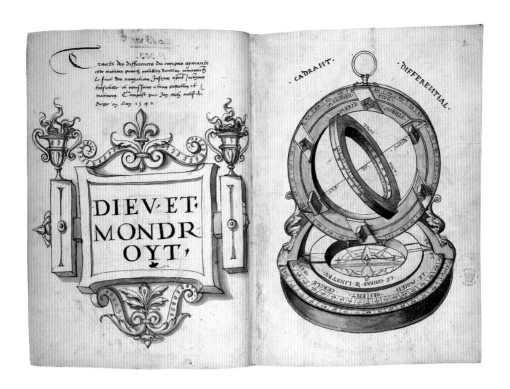

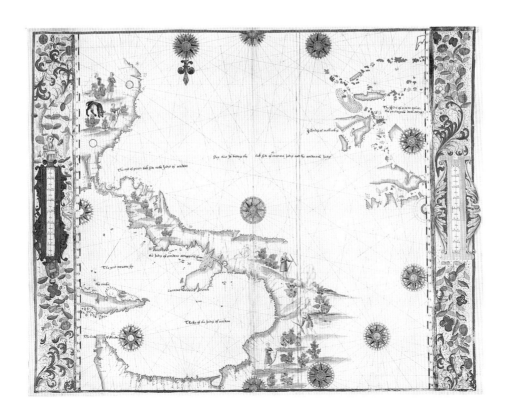

This last example reminds us that by the late 1530s a variety of literal translations of Luther's works from German (rather than covert adaptations in French) had begun to appear in the royal library in spite of Henry's chronic distrust of his old adversary. In the fifteenth century the *Donation of Constantine*, a key document in providing precedent for the pope's immense temporal powers, had been exposed as a forgery by Lorenzo Valla in his *De falso credita et ementita Constantini donatine declamatio*. Luther's own attack on the *Donation* was published in 1537 and almost immediately afterwards Thomas Cranmer, Henry's reforming archbishop, sent the king an anonymous translation entitled 'One of the highe Articles of the most holy Popish Faythe, called *Donatio Constantini*'. (57) In the same year Miles

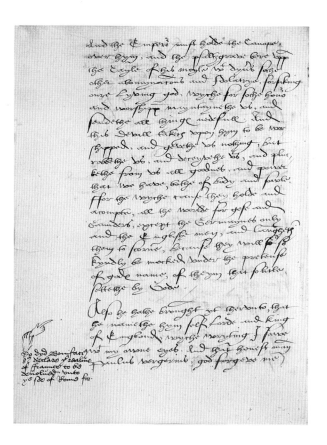

57. In a marginal note to the attack on the *Donatio Constantini* Cranmer has drawn Henry's attention to a passage in which Luther ridiculed the Pope's claim to the lordship of England.
The British Library,
Royal MS 17.C.XI, f. 14 v

Coverdale's translation of Luther's exposition of the Magnificat (Coverdale writing under the alias of John Hollybush) was published at Southwark, and it too survives at Westminster as no. 308 in the inventory, described as 'Exposition upon Magnificat'.

Around 1540 Robert Radcliffe, a grammar-school master at Jesus College Cambridge, presented Henry with three dramatic dialogues translated into English from the Latin *Dialogi aliquot* of the French humanist and rhetorician Jean Tixier de Ravisi, who was arguably the first continental humanist and playwright to influence the English stage. (When the plays

were rediscovered and transcribed in the early decades of the twentieth century they were misattributed to Ralph Radcliffe of Hitchen and were hailed
as the 'missing link between mediaeval and Shakespearian drama'.) One of
these dialogues, 'concernyng a governance of the Chirch', would have
seemed particularly germane in these years of religious revolution and
counter-revolution with its warning: 'beware of false prophetes which come
to you in the clothes of shepe, but inwardly they are ravenous wolfes'. Radcliffe had obtained his teaching position through Cromwell's intervention
just before the latter's fall, and no doubt this manuscript was a token – an
entirely appropriate one for a schoolmaster – of gratitude to his patron's
patron. After it got to the royal library it was bound by King Henry's

58. This is one of the last
examples of the work of
King Henry's Binder, who
had been actively employed
by the crown for more than a
decade. There is no indication
of when or how it left the royal
library.
By permission of Llyfrgell Genedlaethol
Cymru, The National Library of Wales,
MS II.10, cover

Binder with Henry's arms and an HR stamped in gold on the front and
back covers. (58)

One of the most assiduous of Henry's translators was Henry Parker,
eighth baron Morley (c.1481–1556). Although he was connected to the
royal family through marriage and became a close friend of Henry's elder
daughter in the 1530s, Morley was never at the centre of power and has
been described by David Starkey as an attendant lord, in the manner of
T. S. Eliot's J. Alfred Prufrock, rather than a courtier as such. From the late
1520s onwards Morley presented Henry VIII with a manuscript copy of

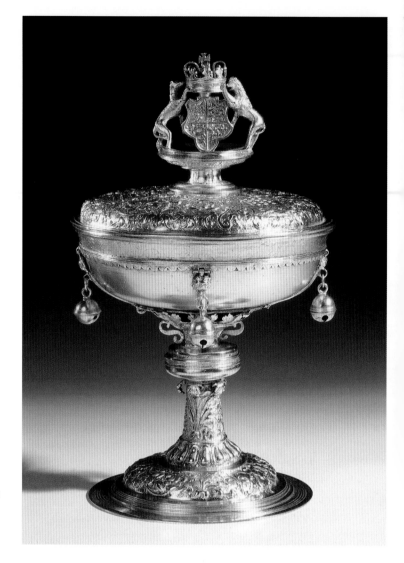

59. Similar to the gifts
received by Morley, although
on a grander scale, this silver
gilt standing cup with cover
was presented by Henry VIII
to the united company of the
Barber Surgeons around 1543.
Tudor roses, fleurs-de-lis and
portcullises, along with Henry's
arms and supporters, identify
the donor.
Courtesy of the Worshipful Company
of Barbers

one of his own works each New Year's Day and received a piece of silver
plate in return, almost inevitably a gilt cup with a cover. (59) He also provided translations of pious works for Lady Mary – for such was the title
conferred on the former princess after the official dissolution of her parents'
marriage – and on occasion for Thomas Cromwell as well. Prefacing each
effort was a flattering letter, and these followed a fairly standard format.
The physical structure of the books was also relatively similar: often written and illuminated by the same group of scribes, they contained fifteen to
forty leaves and normally had three or four historiated initials with scrollwork and animal or grotesque heads. They were not, in other words,
expensive or ostentatious offerings and it was as much a statement of fact
as a rhetorical exercise when Morley requested Henry 'not to regarde the
rudenes' of the gift, but rather to consider 'the faithfulnes of me your

subiect, that wylleth with the very harte, as he writeth, goodnes, and all goodnesse to you'.

One volume, however, stands out dramatically from the others in terms of quality and quantity of illumination. Now at Chatsworth House, this is a translation of forty-six lives from Boccaccio's *De claris mulieribus* presented on New Year's Day 1543: it contains forty-seven leaves and has strapwork initials with scrollwork and grotesques, animals or flowers on almost every leaf. (60) Why, then, did Morley present Henry with such a fine book, well beyond what he could easily afford, on this particular occasion and at no other time in his career?

In the preface to his version of *De claris mulieribus* Morley links Boccaccio's tales to the contemporary world and expresses the hope that the ladies at Henry's court will learn from the examples of their classical predecessors: 'seynge the glorye of the goode [they] may be steryde to folowe theym, and seynge the vyce of sum, to flee theym'. This seems a markedly specific allusion and there is a context. Morley's daughter Jane, Lady Rochford, the widow of Anne Boleyn's brother George, had become Matron of Queen Catherine Howard's Suite in 1540. Taking advantage of her position she acted as a procuress for Catherine and her lover Thomas Culpeper — to whom the young queen, incautious to the point of folly, had written some eight months after her marriage:

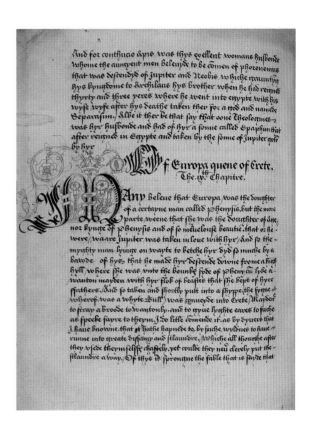

> ytt makes my harte to dye to thynke what fortune I have that I cannot be always yn your company. Yt my trust is allway in you that you wol be as you have promysed me, and in that hope I truste upon styll, prayng you than that you wyll com when my lade Rochforthe ys here, for then I shal be best at leasysoure to be at your commaundment.

The letter is signed: 'Yours as long as lyffe endures, Katheryn'. Once the affair was discovered, both the queen and Lady Rochford, who was described by contemporaries as 'that bawde', and by David Starkey as Nurse to Catherine's Juliet, were condemned to death. Morley himself was present at the time of the attainder. The execution took place on Tower Green on 13 February 1542 and Catherine's speech, as it was reported by an observer, is remarkably similar in sentiment and even in phrasing to Morley's preface: confessing that she had offended God from her earliest youth, she entreated the people 'to take example at [her], for amendment of their ungodly lives and gladly to obey the King in all things'. Jane Rochford's disgrace

60. The crowned M is decorated with the rose and pomegranate, and there are marigolds between the shafts. The combination seems an odd one for the 1540s, since Catherine of Aragon's emblem was the pomegranate and Mary's the marigold.
The Devonshire Collection, Chatsworth, MS, f. 11v

reflected on her whole family and Morley found himself in an extraordinarily vulnerable position. What the translation of *De claris mulieribus* in its luxurious format represents is an encoded repudiation of Jane's actions and an act of submission to Henry. Without actually naming his daughter, Morley tacitly condoned the punishment of female promiscuity no matter who was involved and endorsed the need to control the behaviour of the ladies at court. The Chatsworth manuscript is thus a witness to the absolute power of politics in Tudor court life: like Thomas Boleyn several years earlier, Morley was forced not only to submerge private grief but also to dissociate himself from his own flesh and blood in order to salvage his position and maintain his alliances.

Only on rare occasions were old books passed on to the royal family and when Morley presented Lady Mary with a manuscript of the commentary on the Latin psalter by the fourteenth-century mystic Richard Rolle, he felt compelled to apologize for offering 'suche an olde boke', explaining that the contents alone redeemed it: 'thoughe percase sum that knowythe not what a preciouse thyng ys hyde in thys so rude a letter ... yet that hyghe and exellent wytt of yours wyll in the redynge of this exposition of thys psalter deme all other wyse'. Nevertheless, two of Henry's greatest treasures were ancient manuscripts, both biblical texts and both gifts to him.

The older of these is a magnficently illustrated late-fifth/early-sixth-century copy of the Greek text of Genesis; according to modern commentators this is one of the most influential biblical codices of the Middle Ages. During her reign Elizabeth handed it on to her tutor in Greek and Latin, Sir John Fortescue, and from Fortescue it passed to the seventeenth-century collector Sir Robert Cotton. Although the manuscript was terribly damaged by the horrific fire at Ashburnham House in 1731, scholars have put much effort into reconstruct-ing the text and illustrations. (61) Cotton believed, anachronistically, that it was once owned by the Greek Church father Origen (*c*.185–*c*.254) and that it was given to Henry VIII by Greek bishops visiting from Philippi. In fact, by the thirteenth century it had been transported to Venice, quite likely from Alexandria rather than Philippi, and it was the principal model for the famous atrium mosaics at San Marco. In the tumultuous mid-dle years of Henry's reign, when his agents were pillaging scripture to find a justification for the annulment of his marriage to the long-suffering Cather-ine of Aragon, it was brought to England from Venice – perhaps by the king's cousin Reginald Pole. Later it was acquired by one of Henry's advi-sors on the interpretation of Leviticus, Robert Wakefield, an expert in the *triae linguae* essential to the humanist programme of education (Latin, Greek and Hebrew) and King's reader in Hebrew at Oxford. After Robert's death in 1537 it went to his younger brother Thomas, who became first

61. With sad understatement, post-conflagration accounts described the Cotton Genesis as 'much contracted by fire'. Illustrated here is a relatively undamaged leaf, which shows the angels speaking with Lot, whose left hand is raised in a gesture of beckoning.
The British Library,
Cotton MS Otho B.vi, f. 28r

Regius professor of Hebrew at Cambridge in 1540, and Thomas then presented it to the king along with another work of his own composing, possibly in gratitude for his appointment to the Regius chair.

The second of these biblical texts, the so-called Golden Gospels, is a spectacular book probably written at the Benedictine monastery of St Maximin at Trier during the tenth century in gold letters on heavy vellum stained purple. (62) How did Henry obtain such an important early continental manuscript? In 1521 a handwritten copy bound in cloth-of-gold of Henry's *Assertio septem sacramentorum* was prepared for Pope Leo X in which the following Latin verses were added: 'Henry, king of England, sends this work to Leo X, as a witness of his faith and his friendship'. Henry was, as he had hoped, rewarded with the coveted title of *Fidei defensor* for his scholarship, and it is just possible, as an eighteenth-century owner states, that Leo sent him this magnificent offering into which the matching verses were inserted. By this reading these latter paid tribute to the king's contribution to orthodoxy, which had 'restrengthened the faith' and maintained the true church in the face of the Lutheran threat. There are other possible explanations as well. Whatever else the book was still in the royal library where Sir Robert Cotton's librarian Richard James (1592–1638) saw it and mistakenly identified it as the Gospel book given by St Wilfrid to Ripon and described by Bede in his *Ecclesiastical History*. When precisely it escaped is unknown.

Printed books

Usually less ostentatious than manuscripts, the printed books given to Henry were personalized in a variety of ways. At the lowest end of the spectrum Henry regularly received 'off the rack' imprints, chosen because of appropriateness of topic or occasion. The New Year's gift-roll for 1534, for example, records that John Leland provided the king with two books of stories. No doubt Leland entered a handwritten Latin poem in praise of the king on a flyleaf, perhaps even the set of verses of which he kept a record in one of his notebooks:

In the frontispiece of this little book.

Enter, o book, the laurel-decked hearth
Of the serene King Henry.
Enter and shake off your rustic modesty.
The king will receive you with a gracious hand,
Famous companion of the Muses,
Lively and devout champion of singing Apollo.

Thomas Berthelet gave books at New Year, as was suitable to his position as King's Printer, and so too did the royal schoolmaster Richard Featherstone. On occasion a letter was bound into the book as a permanent reminder of the link between donor and recipient. The humanist scholar and royal physician Thomas Linacre (*c.*1460–1524) presented Henry with a copy of *Paulina de recta Paschae celebratione* (Fossombrone, 1513) by Paulus

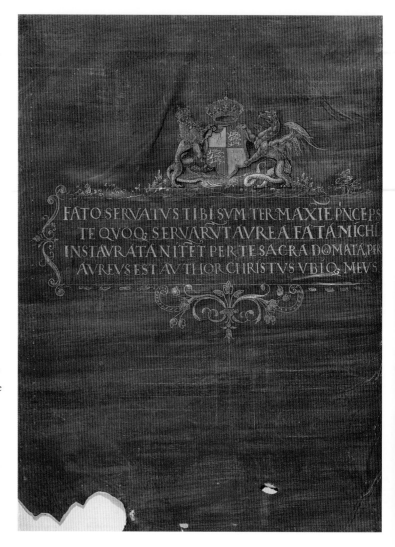

62. The arms of England have been emblazoned on the first leaf of the Golden Gospels. There are also Latin verses which read in translation: 'By fate I have been saved for you, thrice greatest Prince; / The golden fates have also preserved you for me. / The sacred doctrines, restored by you, shine forth. / My golden author, Christ, is known everywhere through you.'
The Pierpont Morgan Library, New York, MS M. 23, f. 1v

de Middelburg, the German mathematician, physician and bishop of Fos-sombrone, who sat on the commission to reform the calendar at the time of the fifth Lateran Council (1512–17). Middleburg, who influenced Nico-las Copernicus, based his arguments for the correct dating of Easter – the focus of the *Paulina* – in part on the speculations of the medieval Oxford philosopher Roger Bacon. Henry's copy, which was bound by the London stationer John Reynes, contains a prefacing letter in Linacre's elegant script. Linacre also sent the king vellum copies of his own works, includ-ing his 1519 translation from Greek to Latin of the classic medical treatise *Methodus medendi* ('The Practice of Medicine') by the ancient Greek physi-cian Galen. (63)

Although he owned a number of translations from Greek to Latin, Henry did not have a large collection of books in the original Greek; one of the few is a copy in four volumes printed on vellum at Verona in 1529 of the

63. Linacre's translation was
elaborately bound for Henry
by the so-called 'Louis XII-
François I' Binder. Linacre
gave another copy, similarly
finished, to Wolsey.
The British Library, C.19.e.17, cover

editio princeps of St John Chrysostom's commentary on the Pauline Epistles,
a text much favoured by Erasmus and other reformers. This edition was
issued by the Venetian printers Nicolini da Sabbio et fratelli under the spon-
sorship of the progressive bishop of Verona, Gian Matteo Giberti
(1495–1542), and formed part of the latter's programme of ecclesiastical
reform based on contemporary ideals of a return to the teachings of the early
church fathers. As well as the standard dedicatory epistle to Pope Clement
VII, Henry's vellum copy is unique in having a second epistle addressed to
the king; what is truly surprising, however, is that it is printed rather than
handwritten. (64) The impression conveyed by this second epistle is that
Henry was a dedicatee along with Clement of the whole print run rather
than of this copy only; he and Clement are linked together as 'the two most
outstanding defenders of the Christian commonwealth and the brightest
lights of our age'. Giberti's motives in this apparent sleight of hand were

SERENISSIMO, ATQVE INVICTISSIMO ANGLIAE
ET FRANCIAE &c. REGI HENRICO VIII FIDEI
DEFENSORI DONATVS VERONENSIS.

OMNES propémodum, Serenißime Rex, quibus quidpiam fcribere ad quempiam ufu
uenit, iftiufmodi & maieftatis & fapientiæ in faftigio collocatum, cuiufmodi es tu, conuue-
uere, occafionem initiumq; fcribendi ab illa Platonis fententia fumere, quæ declarat, tunc
& regna felicia & ciuitates fore, quum aut fapientes homines regnare cœperint, aut ipfi
reges fieri fapientes. ita altius exorfi, omnem huc orationem poftremò deducunt, ut illum ad
quem fcribunt, talis & fuæ & fuorum felicitatis compotem euafiffe demonftrent. Quod fi
illi quidem fyncere & abfque ulla adulationis fufpicione aut fraude ufurpare potuerunt, quos
etiam mediocribus quibufdam id laudis tribuiffe non ignoramus : quanto mihi nunc iuftius idem
fucere liceat? qui quamuis nec ad hoc fcribendi munus admodum idoneus, nec fatis tuæ
maieftati notus, ad te ipfum tamen fcribere iuffus fum : cuius unius tanta eft laus fapientiæ,
ut pronunciare nullo modo audeam, planeq; me nefcire profitear, utrum maius ornamentum ab
altero accipiat, ftudium fapientiæ à regia maieftate, an regia maieftas à ftudio fapientiæ.
ita enim iftic utrunque alteri amicum eft, ita tu ex utroque temperatus, ut vere in uno red-
datur fuauiffimum illud perfectiffimumq; muficæ genus, quod follicite quærens Plato, modo
Aegyptum peragrabat, modo noftram Italiam Siciliamq; vifebat, quem quidem Philofo-
phum non dubito, noftro hoc omni relicto orbe, in iftum alterum, fi modo te iftic imperantem
audiuiffet, primo quoq; tempore uolaturum fuiffe. fed nec in Platone Ariftotele ue potentiam,
nec in Dionyfio, Philippo, aliis ue fapientiam, videre potuit illa ætas : quorum neutrum in te
uno, nec id quidem abfq; fingulari fummi Dei beneficio, hæc noftra defyderat. ac feliciffime
potius utrunque contunctum agnofcit. hoc vere imperare, hoc vere regnare eft : non una via
delicet nobilitate generis, non uno habitu culuq; corporis, non unis diuitiis unà ue potentia, fuis
ciuibus antecellere, quod plerifq; accidit : fed multo etiam magis animi claritate atque opibus,
quod pauciffimis contigit. & eo iuftius hoc te à me teftimonium expectare decet, quod non uul-
garis cuiufpiam fapientiæ, fed illius quæ una vere fapientia dicenda eft, & quam vel illi ipfi,
quos diximus, Plato Ariftotelefq; ignorauerint, ftudium & laudem ubi hoc tempore vendica-
ueris. eam fane dico fapientiam, quam una chriftiana religio docere idonea eft : quæ quum humana omnia contemnat, ac pro nihilo ducat, diuina quæ funt non folum veftigat follicitaq;
quirit, fed etiam fuis fectatoribus fe prætituram facillime pollicetur. hanc tu fapientiam non
ingenio tantum & cognitione & verbis, fed multo etiam illuftrius factis totaq; uita collis atque
amplexaris. Hoc vero poftremum eft, auguftiffime Rex, in quo uno oratio mea non deficere
non poteft. nam quum alii multi & regnauerint, nec honeftarum magnarumq; artium fcientia ca-
ruerint, & ftylo quoque atque eloquentia clari exftiterint. adeo ut fine ulla difficultate omnia quæ-
cunque ipfi geffiffent, monumentis commendare idonei fuerint : (quorum omnium bonorum tem-
tempore fingulari quadam Dei benignitate nullum planè in te uno defyderari videmus :) pau-

64. The second preface to
Chrysostom's commentary, in
italic print, is by the Veronese
scholar Bernardino Donato,
who 'reflects upon this unique
harmony of all the virtues and
marks of honour in such a king
at such a time' and states himself
'convinced that that which
previously seemed incredible
and fabulous is indeed true'
in the person of Henry.
The British Library, C.24. f.1, preface

partially financial. He had come briefly to England earlier in the decade to
drum up support for the campaign of Clement VII (Giulio de' Medici
before his elevation) to succeed the ailing Adrian VI as pope and he had
quickly established a good working relationship with the king and Wolsey.
As a result he was appointed bishop of Worcester in 1524, and this brought
an annual pension of two thousand ducats. Once Henry's mind turned to
the question of the validity of his first marriage both he and his cardinal
assumed that Giberti would act as a friend at the papal court: they were
shocked and dismayed when Giberti withdrew from the curia in 1528 after
the decimating Sack of Rome by Spanish, German and Italian troops in the
previous year, a tragedy for which many considered him responsible. Giberti,
for his part, was loath to declare himself openly for the king and one suspects
that this elegant and unusual presentation represented an attempt to divert

Henry's attention; to show loyalty in an English context, where this copy would be seen, but to remain much more non-committal in Italy, where the book would circulate more generally and without the added dedication.

Henry could not be put off the scent this easily, of course, and he continued to exert pressure on Giberti as the divorce debate became more and more acrimonious. In 1532 Giberti's printers published a set of biblical commentaries in Greek, the *Expositiones antiquae*, attributed to Oecumenius, the tenth-century bishop of Trikka. Once again an added dedication in print was included in the vellum copy dispatched to Henry and the monarch's virtues were conspicuously praised: 'the most generous, the most just and the most invincible, alone surpassing all other kings and princes with the felicity of your character and the wisdom of your mind'. By this time Giberti's basic allegiance to Catherine was becoming apparent, however, and in this same year Sabbio et fratelli issued a spirited defence of the indissolubility of the royal marriage by Ludovico Nogarola, count of Verona, dedicated to Catherine's nephew Charles V. Not surprisingly, Giberti's pension was discontinued soon after this betrayal and in spite of his best efforts it was never reinstated; by 20 April 1537, full of self-pity, the Italian bishop was lamenting that: 'I had always had the greatest love for the king, as the king knew, both when Pope Clement was his friend and when he was the contrary, and his Majesty had written to me with his own hand to go thither.' He was luckier than many of his English counterparts, nevertheless, and at least his head was spared.

Pierfrancesco di Piero Bardi (d. 1534) was a member of a powerful Italian merchant family and a partner in a highly successful London trading company. In his youth, before he left Florence, he came under the influence of Girolamo Savonarola, whose prophecies had electrified the Florentines at the close of the fifteenth century. Savonarola had predicted the conquest of Italy by Charles VIII of France in 1494 and had hailed him as a saviour who would liberate Florence from the twin yokes of emperor and pope. Ultimately Charles disappointed Savonarola, who later violently denounced the French king in public oratory and in his writings. The Florentines, for their part, turned against the prophet and in 1498 Savonarola, along with two of his companions, was burned at the stake. Savonarola's last moments of doubt and fear, his feelings of abandonment, are vividly recreated in George Eliot's *Romola*:

> Savonarola was there. He was not far off her [the eponymous heroine] now. He had mounted the steps; she could see him look round on the multitude. But in the same moment expectation died, and she only saw what he was seeing – torches waving to kindle the fuel beneath his dead body, faces glaring with a yet worse light; she only heard what he was hearing – gross jests, taunts, and curses. The moment was past. Her face was covered again, and she only knew that Savonarola's voice had passed into eternal silence.

It is no wonder that the memory of Savonarola's death stuck deeply in Bardi's consciousness and that it resurfaced in a series of psychic disruptions which he recorded in the margins of two books: his copy of the polyglot or octuplex Psalter published in 1516, now at St John's College Cambridge, (65) and his copy, now at Lambeth Palace, of a strange little book of predictions concerning an emerging world emperor and angelic pope, the *Mirabilis liber*, published in Paris around 1523. After making his annotations Bardi sent both books to Henry VIII, probably at New Year 1531/2.

From Bardi's commentary, in many ways a pastiche of biblical quotations, a narrative can be reconstructed. Bardi describes how in November 1517 – just six months after his relation Francesco de' Bardi had been singled out as

65. *Right* In a very unsteady hand Bardi has inscribed the book: 'Serenissimo regi Anglie et ceterorum Henrico VIII' (For Henry VIII, the most serene king of England &c.).
By permission of the Master and Fellows of St John's College, Cambridge, Tt.3.31, title page

66. *Opposite* In this passage Bardi explains: 'I acted wickedly because I deprived this holy man [Savonarola] of his deserved praise, for although I knew fourteen years ago that he and the two companions burned with him were with Christ I was silent; but the incredulity of others and my imprudence were the causes. I was in my chamber in London in the month of November 1517, and they visited me along with a celestial being named A, as I was reflecting and vigilant in the darkness at midnight. Although I could have done so, I do not wish to say what else I might have seen; it is not proper. I shall not say with Paul "whether in the body or without the body" fourteen years ago, but with bended knees I shall sing from the heart, "Thou hast proved my heart; thou hast visited me in the night" &c.'
Lambeth Palace Library, IJ1815.M5, f. lxvᵛ-lxviʳ

a target in the notoriously anti-Lombard Evil May Day riots by the London apprentices – he was meditating late at night in his chamber when an angelic visitor appeared, assuring him that the Florentine martyrs were with Christ. Concerned about other people's scepticism and fearing mockery, he did not reveal this encounter to anyone; he thus behaved like his biblical namesake at the court of the High Priest. Six years later, in 1523, he acquired a copy of the *Mirabilis liber* which contained Savonarola's *Compendium revelationum*. Reading the text reminded him of his earlier cowardly silence. This in turn led to a breakdown, during which he raved for a matter of months, crying out in the words of Scripture, as had Savonarola himself, 'And, behold, I, even I, do bring a flood of waters upon the earth'. (66) Distracted, he gave a Dominican acquaintance, perhaps his confessor, his copy of the accursed book.

In 1531 while rereading the octuplex Psalter in the light of his examination of the recently published *De occulta philosophiae* by the German cabbalist

humana cognitióe nó diſtā-
tia ꝓpheta percepit: ipſi te ſui luminis ea nouit: eā
nāꝗ lumē qꝃeadmodū aḋ dẻo ſolo accipiūt illa: quibus
uina ſic etiā multo magis ad ipſe reuelare dignaꝰ. In humana ꝑtingere poteſt. A iuſmodi aūt reuelatione nō
cognitióe aūt naturali cutuſꝗ facit. ꝓpio. Quodꝗ lumē
libet creature procul recẻdit ſupꝛnaturale ꝓphete ſꝑunde
futura ꝓtingētia: maximẻ ꝗ ꝗꝗ eſt ꝗꝗas participatio lu-
a libero arbitrio vꝛpẻdẻt ꝗ etᵘitatis. Et quo i reueli
ſeipſis neꝗ ab hoibus neꝗ tionibus dẻum ꝓpheta duoꝝ
ab alia creatura ſciri poſſunt ſcernit: eſt eſt ꝗ ipſa reueli
Soli em trinitati tẻpus oſſe ta vera ſunt: ꝗ a dẻo ꝓdu
complectenti preſentia ſunt muūt Tātẻ ꝗꝛo efficacẻ hẻc
Rurſus, a creatura rationali lumen ꝗ dẻuoꝛ ꝓducens
vel itellectuali in eoꝛ cauſẻ ita certū facit prophetāẻ
cognoſci nequeūt. Cū enim lumẻ naturale certos redd
ipſe cauſe indifferẻtẻs ſūt aḋ philoſophos ḋe veritate ꝓ
producẻdosvel nó ad produ motū principioꝛᵘ: ꝗ quiḋet
cẻdos eiuſmodi effectus có hominẻ ꝗ ḋis duo ſit quā
tingētẻs: nó poteſt creatus i tuoꝛ. Secūḋo diſtinctẻ, ꝓ
tellectus diſcernere in quam nit ꝓphete quicquid illi ơꝔ
partem ipſe cauſe inclinatæ gnoſcere ꝓ ceteras Ita
ſūt. Quæobꝛ oꝛ diuinatiō dit: ꝗ hoc m̄timoḋe effict
rie artes: ꝗꝛᵘ ꝑceps Aſtro cut ſcriptū ẻ Oſee.i. cuꝛ
nomia iudicialis habẻt a ḋi lo: Locutus ſum ſuꝑ ꝓphe
uinis ſcripturis ꝗ ḋ eccleſia tas: et ego viſiōnem multipl
ſticis canonibus ḋānate ſūt. cauit: in manu ꝓphetaꝛ
Cognoſcere ſiquiḋẻ contin aſſimulatus ſum. Interḋum
gẻtia futura ſapiẻtẻ diuinẻ abſꝗ imaginaria viſione ĩn
ꝓpuil eſt: coāꝗ omnia tellectu prophete ĩnꝓꝛataẻ
preterita preſentia ẻ futura hūiciure ḋebeat: quô Salo
ſimul aſtantiſicut ſcriptū eſt. moni ſapiẻtia iñfuḋit. Et
Omnia ſunt nuḋa ẻ aperta taliter Daviḋ ꝓphet.aut. In
oculis eius. Nõ poſſunt igt terḋū in imaginatione ḋiuer
tur futura contingẻtia aliꝗ ſas figuras ẻ imaginaꝛᵘ
lumine naturali perpendi ꝑe ſtiones imprimit: que ſignifi

cant iḋ quoḋ intelligere ẻ pre
nunciare ad ꝓphetā ſpectat:
ꝗe aūt propheta ẻ virtute
auiſḋe luminis aperte intelli-
git ſignificationes eiuſcemo-
ḋi viſionum. Aliter propheta
ḋicion poſſet. Vnḋe Danie-
lis.x.capitulo ſcriptū eſt: intel
ligẻtia opus eſt iñ viſione. Se
pe auẻ in talibus viſionibus
iñtrinſecus pronunciari ḋiuer
ſa verba percipit a ḋiuerſis
perſonis mẻti ſue oblatis: que
per oculos iñtellectuales magnifi-
candarum rerum ḋeus ꝓpo
nit. vt Danielis.v.capitulo le
gitur ḋe manuꝗ in pariete
ſcribẻtis iñſcripſit Mane. Tethel.
Phares.que oculis corporis
Daniel quoꝗ viḋit ẻ interno
lumine interpretatus eſt. No
tandum eſt autem quoḋ has
exteriores apparitiones nec
non ẏmaginarias: deus ange
lico myniſterio efficit: vt iñqt
ſanctus Dionyſius in libro de
celeſti Hierarchia: quia qꝙ-
quiḋ a ḋeo eſt:ordinate proce
ḋit:ẻ ꝗue illud Apoſtoli. Que
a ḋeo ſunt ordinata ſunt. Or
ḋo aūt ḋiuine ſapiẻtie eſt dẻ
ſponere iñfima per media: et
media per ſuprẻma.Cum igt
tur inter ḋeum ẻ hoies angeli
meḋy ſint:ab ipſo ḋeo illumi
tiones propherice per angeli
cos ſpiritus ſubminiſtratur ꝗ
non tantū ad ḋiuerſas apparĩ
tiones iñterius fantaſiam il
luſtrant ẻ commouẻt: ſed etiā
iñtrinſecus ꝓphetas alloqui
tur. Quibus etiam ſepenume
ro exterius ſe in humana figu
ra exhibẻt futura prenuncia
tes ẻ de multis pagẻdis eos
iñſtruentes ẻ per lumen ſupra
dictum. ꝓphete aperte cogno
ſcunt eas apparitiḋes eſſe an
gelozᵘ ẻ ea que iḋem ange
li loquuntur eſſe veraces a ſa
pientia ḋiuina emanare. His
tribus modis quandoꝗ vno
quandoꝗ alio:nos futura ha
buimus ẻ cognouiᵘ. Quo-
quo tamẻ eorum modo ea aḋ
me peruenerit: ſemper ſupra
dicto lumine illuſtrante veriſ
ſima ẻ certiſſima fuiſſe intelle
xi. Proſpiciens itaꝗ omni
potens ḋeus Italie peccata
preſertim in principibus tam
eccleſiaſticis ꝗ Secularibus
multiplicari: Nec ea ḋiutius
ferre valens:ſtatuit eccleſiam
ſuam iñgẻti flagello lo expiare
Et quoniam:vt iñquit Amos
propheta: nó faciet domĩᵘ

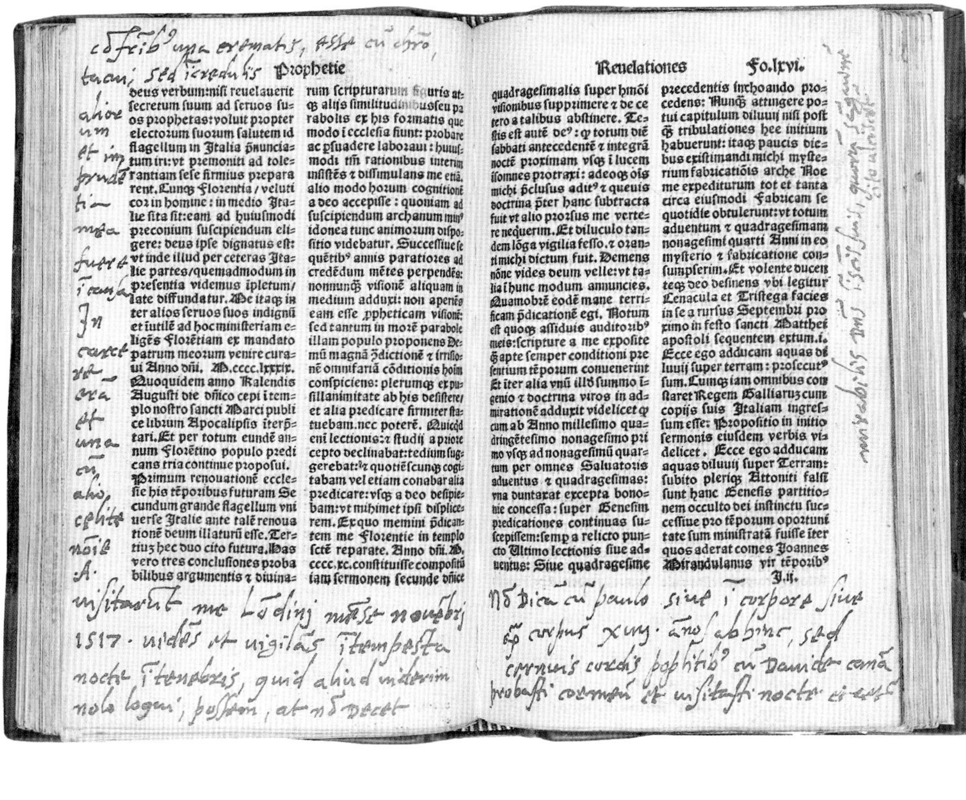

J.i.

[marginalia, manuscript:]
Creati eſtote igitur pauli
Inique agi ꝗm ſcum hīc iñ iꝛᵘ myrſita
Lauḋe fraudulani nā cū ſoiā XIIIĵ
āꝛ̃a ab hīc hūc cū illiſ duobuſ eius

[marginalia, manuscript top:]
cõſcribª uꝛa exematᵗ, fïſſa cū ẻgro,
terani, ſed iñcrediᵇⁱᵘ

ḋeus verbum:niſi reuelauerit
ſecretum ſuum ad ſeruos ſu
os prophetas:voluit propter
electorum ſuorum ſalutem iḋ
flagellum in Italia iminenẻ
turi iri:vt premoniti ad tole
rantiam ſeſe firmius prepara
rent,Cumꝗ Florẻtia / veluti
cor in homine : iñ medio Ita
lie ſita ſit:eam aḋ huiuſmodi
preconium ſuſcipiendum eli
gere: ḋeus ipſe dignatus eſt:
vt inde illud per ceteras Ita
lie partes:quemadmodum iñ
preſentia videmus ipletum:
late diffundatur. Me itaꝗ iſ
ter alios ſeruos ſuos indignū
et iñutile ad hoc miniſteriam e
ligens Florẻtiam ex mandato
patrum meorum venire cura
ui Anno ḋñi. M. cccc.lxxxii.
Quoquidem anno Kalendis
Auguſti ḋie vñico cepi i tem
plo noſtro ſancti Marci publi
cẻ librium Apocalipſis iñter̄
tari.Et per totum eunḋ an
num Florẻtino populo predi
cans tria continue propoſui.
Primum renouarioni eccle
ſie his ẻporibus futuram Se
cundum grande flagellum vni
uerſe Italie ante talẻ renoua
tiōnẻ morū illaturi eſſe.Ter
tiuᵒ hec duo cito futura.Has
vero tres concluſiones ꝓba
bilibus argumentis ẻ ḋiuina

quadrageſimalis ſuper hmöi
viſionibus ſupprimere ẻ ce
tero a talibus abſtinere. Te
ſtis eſt aut ḋeᵒ: ꝗ totum ḋiẻ
ſabbati antecedentẻ ẻ integra
nocte proximam vſꝗ i lucem
ſomnes protraxi: adeoꝗ ois
michi ſclusus aḋit ꝗ queuis
doctrina ſter hanc ſubtracta
fuit et alio proꝛſus me verte
re nequerim.Et ḋiluculo tan
dem lõga vigilia feſſo. ẻ orā
ti michi ḋictum fuit. Demens
nõne vides ḋeum velle:vt ta
lia hunc modum annuncies.
Quamobꝛ eõḋe mane terri
ficam ꝓḋicationem egi, Notum
eſt quoꝗ aſſidue auḋitoribᵘ
meis:ſcripture a me expoſite
ꝗ apte ſemper conditioni pre
ſentium ẻporum conuenerint
Et iter alia vñ illô ſummo i
genio ẻ doctrina viros iñ aḋ
miratione aḋḋuxit videlicet q
cum ab Anno milleſimo qua
ḋringenteſimo nonageſimo pri
mo vſꝗ ad nonageſimū quar
tum per omnes Saluatoris
aḋuentus ẻ quadrageſimas:
vna buntaur excepta bono
nie conceſſa: ſuper Genẻſim
predicationes continuas ſu
ſcepiſſem:ſemꝗ a relicto pun
cto Ultimo lectionis ſiue aḋ
uentus: Siue quadrageſimẻ

precedentis iñchoando pro
cedens: Nunꝗ attingere po
tui capitulum diluuii niſi poſt
ꝗ tribulationes hec inicium
habuerunt: itaꝗ paucis die
bus exiſtimandi michi myſte
rium fabricatiōis arche Noe
me expediturum tot et tanta
circa eiuſmodi fabricam ſe
quotidie obtulerunt:vt totum
aḋuentum ẻ quadrageſimam
nonageſimi quarti Anni in eo
myſterio ẻ fabicatione con
ſumpſerim.Et volente ḋucẻ
teꝗ ḋeo deſinens vbi legitur
Lenacula et Triſtega facies
iñ ſe a rurſus Septembui pro
ximo in feſto ſancti Matthei
apoſtoli ſequentem extum.i.
Ecce ego aḋḋucam aquas ḋe
luuii ſuper terram: proſecut
ſum,Cumꝗ iam omnibus con
ſtaret Regem Galliarum cum
copiis ſuis Italiam iñgreſ
ſum eſſe: ꝓpoſitio in initio
ſermonis eiuſdem verbia viꝛ
delicet, Ecce ego aḋḋucam
aquas ḋiluuii ſuper Terram:
ſubito pleriꝗ Attoniti falſẻ
ſunt hanc Geneſis partitio
nem occulto ḋei iñſtinctu ſuc
ceſſiue pro ẻporum oportuni
tate ſum miniſtrata fuiſſe iter
quos aḋerat comes Joannes
Mirandulanus vir ẻporibᵘ

J.ii.

[marginalia right, manuscript:]
non vidbi.lxⱽ ẘꝰ lᵗ ſcribᵃⁿ quactᵃ ꝗ garitᵘᵃ
ſtiḋ alꝛaſiᵇⁱ

[marginalia bottom, manuscript:]
uiſitauit me Loḋij mẻſe nouẻbris
1517. uiḋes et uigilas iñtempeſta
noctẻ iñtenebris, quid aliud uiderim
nolo loqui; poſſem, at nõ ḋecet

nõ ḋicā cū paulo   ſiue i corpore ſiue
ꝗ archuᵐ XIIIĵ ãno ab hinc, ſed
cernis corde ꝗphitiᵒ cū Daviḋe canā
probaſti cremari et uiſitaſti noctᵘ cõ exͭ

and demonologist Cornelius Agrippa, he saw the significance of his revela-
tion and also realized that there was an analogy between the foolish behaviour of the English in the present crisis over the king's marital status and the
equally stupid actions of the Florentines at the end of the previous century.
At this point he began to glimpse a solution for the problems besetting both
the Florentines and the English and he therefore set about getting back the
Mirabilis liber. Once rescued, this book led him to his own fully fledged rev-
elation, which he carefully recorded in its margins. He now realized that
exactly fourteen years after his original angelic visitation the meaning of
present and past events were being revealed to him; he understood himself
to be in the identical position to the man whom St Paul described in
2 Corinthians 12:4: 'I knew a man in Christ above fourteen years ago
(whether in the body, I cannot tell; or whether out of the body, I cannot tell:
God knoweth); such an one caught up to the third heaven… How that he
was caught up into paradise, and heard unspeakable words, which it is not
lawful to speak.'

Mimicking the very language of St Paul, Bardi took on the mantle of a
Savonarola *redivivus*, advising a potential Charles VIII *redivivus*. Address-
ing himself to Henry through his marginalia – there is no evidence he had a
personal audience with the king – he pointed out that a *Fidei defensor*, such as
Henry, could be elected to the required task where a mere most Christian
king (i.e. the French Charles VIII) had failed. And what was the task?
What was Henry meant to do? And why did he receive these books covered
in cryptic commentary? In 1530 a beleaguered Florence had surrendered to
Catherine's nephew, the Holy Roman Emperor Charles V, and Pope
Clement VII. In 1531 Charles declared Alessandro de' Medici head of the
government in Florence. For patriots like Bardi this appeared a disaster, a
replay of the events of the early 1490s. What Bardi wished, therefore, was
that Henry would assume the heroic mantle and save Florence in a manner
that Charles VIII had failed to do. To persuade the king, he emphasized the
parallels between the plight of the Florentines, oppressed by pope and
emperor, and Henry himself, oppressed by the same forces. Implicitly, therefore, he was offering a solution to the present crisis, one revealed, so he insin-
uated, mystically, and one which would serve the Florentines too. As is the
case with most prophets, however, his was a voice crying in the wilderness
and it was not heard.

Books dedicated to the king and commissioned works

Most books dedicated to Henry came from scholars either seeking patronage
or showing gratitude for favours received: the royal library contained a presentation copy of the revised version dedicated to Henry of the German
reformer Philipp Melanchthon's *Loci communes rerum theologicarum* ('General
Arguments on Theological Matters') – a text about which Henry's opinion
had changed radically between editions – Erasmus's paraphrase of Luke,
Sir Richard Morison's translation of the Roman administrator Frontinus's
Strategemata as *The Strategies, Sleights, and Policies of War*, Juan Luis Vives's
De Europae dissidiis et bello Turcico ('On the Discords of Europe and the

Turkish War'), and Robert Whittinton's edition and translation of Cicero's *De officiis* ('On Duties').

Sir Thomas Elyot dedicated several works to Henry, including his Latin–English Dictionary (London, 1538) and his *The Image of Governance* (London, 1541). Scrambling for patronage after Wolsey's fall, he produced his earlier *The Boke Named the Governour* (1531) specifically to impress the king with his abilities as a potential counsellor. John Leland's most famous offering to Henry was an unusual one: conceived as a New Year's gift for 1546 it was a short tract, subsequently annotated and printed by John Bale as *The laboryouse Journey & serche of Johan Leylande for Englandes Antiquitees*, outlining the great works Henry's self-proclaimed *antiquarius* planned to write for the king over the next years. His timing was not good; the next year the king died and he himself became permanently insane, none of his grandiose schemes achieved. Two years earlier, in 1544, Leland did publish a polemical tract, the *Assertio inclytissimi Arturii regis Britanniae* (translated in Elizabeth's reign as *The Assertion of K. Arthure*) supporting the historicity of Henry's supposed heroic ancestor. Another lengthy prose work, the *Antiphilarchia*, was cast as a dialogue between a reformer and a Romanist over the *Tu es Petrus* text. Completed after Henry assumed the kingship of Ireland in 1541, it has never been published, but what was no doubt the presentation copy survives as Cambridge University Library, MS Ee.V.14. Leland also compiled a tribute – published some five years after the actual event – to the birth of Prince Edward, the *Genethliacon illustrissimi Eäduerdi principis Cambriae*. (67)

Peter Bienewitz (1495–1552), who Latinized his name to Apianus ('belonging to bees') in a typical humanist conceit, was Professor of Mathematics and Imperial Mathematician to the German Emperor Charles V. He was the first to use darkened glass for observation of the sun, and noted that the tails of comets always point away from it. His *Astronomicum Caesareum* (which he had privately printed at Ingolstadt in 1540), consists of a beautifully illustrated exposition of Ptolemaic astronomy, and is the last major work of its kind to be published before the appearance of Copernicus's *De revolutionibus*. (69) According to a letter written to Henry in 1544 by Nicholas Wotton, ambassador and dean of Canterbury Cathedral, Apianus planned to present Henry, known to have an interest in mathematics, with one of the only seventeen printed copies of the text. Esther Mourits, who is cataloguing the Bibliotheca Thysiana in Leiden, has recently found this copy, bound in leather with Henry's initials: bought by Johannes Thysius at auction in October 1649 in The Hague, it was no doubt one of the books liberated from the royal library at the time of Charles I's fall.

In the preface to his English translation of the chronicles of Jean Froissart, Sir John Bourchier, Lord Berners (*c.*1467–1533), stated that he had undertaken the project at the request of the king himself. (68) Originally written at the time of the Hundred Years' War by a Frenchman at the court of Edward III, Froissart's history – which remains a key document for an understanding of this conflict – was highly popular in the Middle Ages, and many deluxe illuminated manuscripts survive, possibly including the one left to Henry VIII by his grandmother Lady Margaret. Five printed

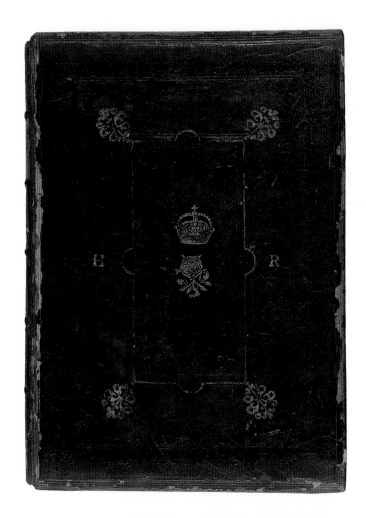

67. *Above* Printed on vellum the presentation copy
of Leland's *Genethliacon illustrissimi Eäduerdi principis
Cambriae* is still in an early binding: there is, on both
front and back covers, a Tudor rose surmounted by
the royal crown within a frame stamped in gold and
ER at the margins. It was abstracted from the royal
library by one Roland Kenrick, who was an employee
of the Court of Augmentations during the 1550s.
By kind permission of the Master, Fellows and Scholars of
Clare College, Cambridge, O 6 26, cover

68. *Right* Berners's portrait, formerly attributed to
Holbein, but in fact painted by an unknown Flemish
artist, hangs in the National Portrait Gallery.
National Portrait Gallery, 4953

69. The hand-finished title page
of the *Astronomicum Caesareum*
includes the figure of the dragon
in its complex and mysterious
design.
The British Library,
Maps C.7.c.15, title page

editions of the French original were issued before 1520 and the work took on
a new resonance for the English after the signing of the Treaty of Bruges in
1521, at which time Henry pledged to declare war on France the following
year. Conceived in two volumes, Berners's translation was intended to
remind 'noble gentlemen' of their ancient right to France and to spur them
on to bravery by enabling them 'to see, behold, and read the high enterprises,
famous acts, and glorious deeds done and achieved by their valiant ancestors'. The first volume, completed in 1522, was issued by the King's Printer,
Richard Pynson, on 28 January 1523. According to its colophon the second
was finished on 10 March 1525 and was printed on 31 August, the day after
the treaty to end the war with France was signed, to which it could be seen as
a coda. (70)

By nature publication renders texts more widely available and the printing
press functioned as an agent for persuasion and propaganda in the sixteenth

70. Berners's Froissart is one
of only three books in which
Pynson's arms appear and their
inclusion may indicate that the
King's Printer shared in the
cost of publication.
The British Library,
G6242, last leaf verso

century. Learned works from the past were regularly translated into the vernacular to increase their accessibility and to emphasize their relevance to contemporary situations. One such, Marsiglio of Padua's *Defensor pacis* ('The Protector of Peace'), completed in 1324, questioned papal authority (the pope is seen as a tyrant, and a usurper), arguing that in ecclesiastical matters a General Council had the real title to supreme authority. The jurisdiction of the pope and the priesthood should be limited, according to Marsiglio, to the administration of the sacraments and the teaching of divine law. This work, of which the *editio princeps* was published in Basel in 1522, hugely appealed to Henry as he set about throwing off papal domination, and Thomas Cromwell financed the first English translation – published in 1535 as *The Defence of Peace* – by William Marshall, one of his stable of authors. After it was printed, the text having been significantly manipulated to reflect contemporary policies, Marshall distributed twenty-four copies to notoriously conservative monks of the London Charterhouse, who consented to consult it only if they were licensed by their president. Three days later all but one copy were returned: this latter was kept by Dom. John Rochester who soon afterwards burnt it, so disgusted was he by what he saw in it – the pope, for example, described as 'the great dragon, and olde serpente anty-chryste of Rome'. Henry's own copy, now lost, of the earlier 1522 imprint was recorded in the 1542 inventory.

On 13 June 1532 Cromwell sent Henry an unidentified book which the 'Friar Carmelite' had brought him that morning. The Carmelite in question was the Italian Giacomo Calco, who had first come to England in 1529. In 1530 he travelled on the king's business to Paris, and managed to obtain a judgment in the king's favour from the University of Paris. In the same year he composed a treatise, *Super diuorcio regis Anglie*, which so impressed the monarch that the King Henry's Binder was commissioned to enclose it in a particularly fine binding, the square central panel of which contains a crowned Tudor rose flanked by fleurs-de-lis and roses. The *Super diuorcio* anticipates the official, and seminal, *Grauissimae academiarum censurae* in the authorities it cites and the way it is organized. Most importantly, it argues that one must obey the voice of one's conscience even at the risk of excommunication, that the internal Catholic church may not always be identical with the instititutional Church of Rome. The *Super diuorcio* is thus the first tract to hint that a break with Rome might be the only way for Henry to untie the Gordian knot confronting him in the person of his unyielding Spanish wife. Now in a private collection it stands in some sense as a foundation charter for the English national church and it is no wonder that there was a large public resistance when the owner applied for (and ultimately obtained) an export licence in 2001.

Multiple copies of recently printed books, including commissioned works, were purchased for the royal libraries and also for distribution. Often the bills included binding expenses and the agent was usually a printer, most regularly the King's Printer. Records of some accounts are found in the surviving Privy Purse expenses, but these are for the most part vague, as in the case of 'divers' printed books delivered to York Place and Hampton Court by the newly appointed King's Printer, Thomas Berthelet, on 31 December 1530. Fortunately, one itemized bill, covering the years 1541–43, has survived and it lists one hundred and twenty-three items, at a 'summa totalis' of one hundred seventeen pounds, six pence ha'penny. (72) A goodly sum was spent on binding, including dos-à-dos bindings, in which a pair of originally discrete texts share a middle board but have opposing spines. (Books were normally sold without bindings at this period and purchasers often bound together several texts, thus creating in some sense their own compendia on a given topic. This represents, then, a continuation of the medieval practice of copying a variety of works into one 'commonplace' book.) Acts

71. Bound in Italy in gold-tooled red morocco this blank book contains twenty 16-leaf quires of paper. It has the HR monogram and Tudor rose opposite the royal arms.

The British Library,
Tab. 1281b.1, pastedown and facing leaf, and cover

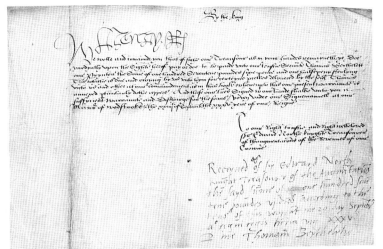

72. The warrant for payment of a bill for books, signed by Henry VIII, was addressed to Sir Edward North, Chancellor of the Court of Augmentations. Berthelet himself acknowledged receipt of payment five days after the warrant was signed.
The British Library,
Addit. MS 28196, ff. 2v–3r

and proclamations – the proclamation for prohibiting hawking, say, or *An acte for foulinge of clothes in Northwales* – were purchased in great quantity, sometimes several hundred copies. Usually there was good reason: for example the thirty-six copies of the declaration against the Scots were delivered to the Principal Secretary, Thomas Wriothesley (whose name is spelt phonetically as Wrysley), during the weeks just before the 'rough wooing' and rout of the Scots at the Battle at Solway Moss late in 1542. Some books simply consisted of blank paper elegantly bound with the king's monogram and other insignia. (71) (In 1531 one Peter Scryvener was paid four pounds for 'bying vellem and other stuf for the kinges bookes'.) Presumably the twelve copies bound in 'paper bordes' or 'forrelles' of the recently printed *Summaria in Euangelia et Epistolas*, originally composed in the ninth century by Smaragdus of Saint-Mihiel, were intended for members of the committee of clerics engaged on revising the Great Bible. For himself Henry ordered a copy bound in white goatskin with a Tudor rose surmounted by a royal crown stamped in gold: this survives in the York Minster library. Likewise, Henry took half a dozen copies of the edition and translation of Cicero's *De officiis* which Robert Whittinton had dedicated to him: five, no doubt meant for the royal schoolroom, were bound in pasteboard but Henry's own was 'gorgiously gilted'. In 1543, hot off the press, came three lots, each containing twenty-four copies, of the so-called 'King's Book', which outlined the most up-to-date views on orthodoxy and was entitled *A necessary doctrine and erudition for any Christen man, sette furth by the kynges majestie*. The price – 'not to be solde above xvi d' for quartos 'bounded in paper bourdes or in claspes' – was printed at the back of the books themselves.

In Henry's reign there were an unusually large number of treason trials, especially after November 1534 when the First Succession Act and the Treason Act were passed, giving the king greater powers to seize property. As we shall see in the case of the Boleyns, Henry often appropriated the books of individuals who tumbled off Fortune's wheel. The biggest cache came in the aftermath of the Wolsey débâcle. Soon after 1527 agents acting for Wolsey, Henry's lord chancellor and chief minister, had begun scouring English monasteries for books which might have a bearing on the king's Great Matter (as the king's marriage crisis was called) and by the time Wolsey died in 1530, at least thirty-one of these had been gathered up into his collection from a variety of monasteries, all identified by a characteristic TC monogram, almost certainly standing for Thomas Cardinalis. (73) For the most part they deal with theology and English history – this is not surprising since the group was assembled as the limits of papal authority were being redefined. One is a copy of Ralph of Flaix's commentary on Leviticus, a text much in demand in these years, since it argued against marriage to a brother's widow. This was based on Leviticus 18:16 and 20:21, where it is stated that: 'You shall not uncover the nakedness of your brother's wife', and 'If a man shall take his brother's wife, it is an impurity… They shall be childless.'

Another of Wolsey's monastic manuscripts is a copy of the homilies of Ælfric of Eynsham, one of the most learned scholars of the late Anglo-Saxon period: the script dates to the late tenth century and the lifetime of Ælfric himself. (74) This is an unexpected text for Wolsey to have owned – he would not have been able to read the Old English, although the Latin headings would have given clues – and perhaps it was chosen because it also contained a Latin version of the apocyphal Gospel of Nicodemus, describing Christ's descent into hell, or perhaps it came in with other manuscripts as part of a 'job lot'.

Works were dedicated to Wolsey by innumerable hopeful clients including Erasmus and more typical of his collection are two surviving presentation manuscripts. Written in Germany and dated 8 June 1524, one is a copy in Latin of the *Mystocryptice* of a certain Luderus de Reventlo, who described himself rather grandly as 'palatinus lateralis, comes ac miles, archiatros, astrotheoricus' (palatine companion, count and knight, physician and astrologer). A mystical cosmographical treatise which has never been published, the *Mystocryptice* is accompanied by complex diagrams to help illuminate the text. (75) Although the correct title in Greek is given on the title page, the individual cataloguing the 1542 inventory, obviously unfamiliar with this language, got his information wrong, believing it to consist of 'Questiones de uirtutibus et uitiis' ('*Quaestiones* on the Virtues and Vices'); he based this conclusion on a scrap from an older vellum cover inserted in the book. (This provides a good indication of the lack of working knowledge

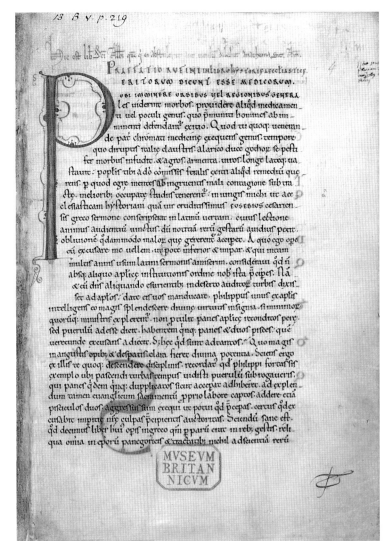

73. At least ten of the manuscripts containing the TC monogram derive from the Benedictine monastery at St Albans, of which Wolsey held the abbacy *in commendam* from 1521.

The British Library,
Royal MS 13.B. v, f. 4

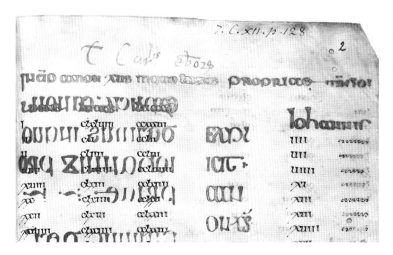

74. In this manuscript Wolsey has signed himself as archbishop of York as well as Cardinal, 'T. Cardinalis Eboracensis'.

The British Library,
Royal MS 7.C.xii, f. 2r

of Greek in the professional circles of Henry's court.) The second presentation manuscript is a verse encomium for New Year 1529 by an unnamed
supplicant. Full of flowery tributes it is conceived as a prophecy of Wolsey's
career (like many prophecies actually retrospective) put in the mouth of the
Roman deity associated with the New Year: it culminates with an account
of Wolsey's accession to the See of Winchester, an appointment that would
have been known in December 1528 when the
poem was written, although the bulls were not
obtained until the following February. (76)

After Wolsey's death Henry may have
obtained two of his disgraced cardinal's most
magnificent books, an illuminated Gospel
Lectionary and Epistolary which were executed as a matched pair. Written by Pieter
Meghen and illuminated by an artist now
known as the Master of Cardinal Wolsey, the
Epistolary is now at Christ Church Oxford
– appropriately, since this is the successor to
Wolsey's projected Oxford college – and the
Gospel book at Magdalen College. These are
the only known English Gospel and Epistle
lectionaries to survive as a pair and they contain
magnificent illuminations, a number identifying their intended owner through motto, arms
or initials. (78–79)

Thomas Linacre presented king and cardinal with his translations into Latin of two
works by the ancient Greek medical writer
Galen, whose authority was still accepted well
into the early modern period. Wolsey's copies
on vellum of the *De sanitate tuenda* ('Hygiene'),
which was dedicated to Henry (Paris, 1517),
and the *Methodus medendi* ('The Practice of
Medicine') (Paris, 1519) still survive. (63)

75. This diagram from the
Mystocryptice illustrates the
Ptolemaic universe with the
earth at the centre.
The British Library,
Royal MS 12.F. XVI, f. 4r

Each has a handwritten dedication to Wolsey and both have been bound, no
doubt at Linacre's expense, in France at the so-called 'Louis XII–François
I' bindery. In 1518 Wolsey lent his assistance to Linacre in the establishment
of the Royal College of Physicians and the publication of the two Galen
translations bracket this event – the first volume was no doubt given as a
supplicatory gesture and the second in token of gratitude. Linacre, who
founded chairs in Greek medicine at Oxford and Cambridge, also directed his
translation of Galen's *De pulsuum usu* ('On the Use of the Pulse'), published in
London in 1523/4, to Wolsey, but the presentation copy has disappeared.

Sylvester Dario, who was papal collector in England and another of
Wolsey's clients, dedicated a treatise on civil law to Wolsey as chancellor; the
work was printed by Pynson in 1521 and the presentation copy to Wolsey
found its way into Henry's library, as did Wolsey's copy of Peter Swawe's

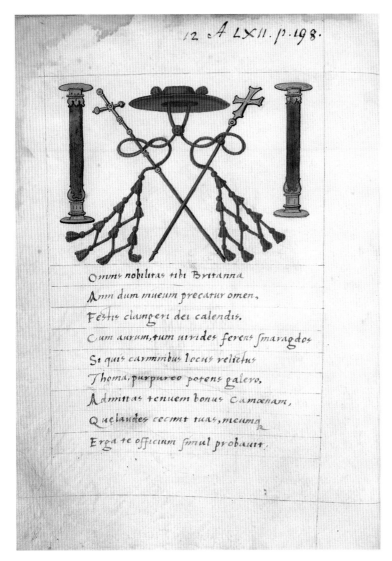

12 A LXII. p.198.

Omnis nobilitas tibi Britanna
Anni dum mueum precatur omen,
Festus clangeri dei calendis.
Cum aurum, tum urides ferens smaragdos
Si quis carmmibus locus relictus
Thoma, purpureo potens galero,
Admittas tenuem bonus Camœnam,
Quelaudes cecini tuas, meuma
Erga te officium simul probauit,

76. The text is surmounted by an illuminated device consisting of a cardinal's hat and crossed croziers between two pillars.
The British Library,
Royal MS 12.A.LXII, f. IV

Serenissimi domini D. Friderici Daniae Noruegiae regis ad Christierni Patruelis calumnias responsio ('Response of the most sereene lord Frederick, king of Denmark and Norway to the Calumnies of Christiernus Patruel'), pub‚ lished at Wittenberg in 1526. This latter has been rebound but there is a modern note linking it with Wolsey: 'TW at foot of original binding' and there is a handwritten inscription to Wolsey in a contemporary hand.

The conservative theologian Cuthbert Tunstall (1474–1559) was bishop of London from 1522, and of Durham from 1530. One of Wolsey's most trusted diplomats, he presented his patron with a copy on vellum of his oration in praise of marriage, *In laudem matrimonii oratio*, pub‚ lished in 1518 on the occasion of the engagement of Princess Mary to the Dauphin. Now in the Bodleian Library, Wolsey's copy, bound for Arch‚ bishop Richard Bancroft after he obtained it from the royal library in the early seventeenth century, has Wolsey's arms and his cardinal's cap inserted on the title page.

In the mid-fifteenth century the Austin friar John Capgrave put together a compendium of the lives of the English saints, the *Noua legenda Angliae* ('New Legends of England') based on the earlier *Sanctilogium* of John of Tynemouth. After its printing in 1516 by Wynkyn de Worde it enjoyed a great popularity and Wolsey's copy of the *editio princeps* is now at Merton College Oxford. It is inscribed to Wolsey as Cardinal of St Cecilia, legate and chancellor; the life of St Thomas Becket was excised at some point after the break with Rome. Whether it was ever sequestered to the royal library is unknown, as is how it got to Merton. Another of de Worde's publications, this one from 1519, was a volume of poetry by the humanist grammarian Robert Whittinton. Much of the verse consisted of praise for Wolsey, and Whittinton had a manuscript version made up of the pertinent sections for the cardinal's delectation. Whittinton was a stylish writer, best known nowadays for his description of Thomas More as 'a man for all seasons', but what sets the manuscript presentation text apart are its covers, the earliest surviving example of English gilt leather binding. (77)

77. The calf covers of this manuscript of Whittinton's poetry have been blocked in gold with two wooden panels: one represents St George and the other the Tudor emblems – rose, portcullis and pomegranate.
Bodleian Library,
Oxford, Bodley MS 523, cover

Contemporary references make it clear that Thomas Cromwell, Wolsey's successor as Henry's principal advisor, had a large collection of books, but their subsequent fate is uncertain. After Wolsey's fall, George Boleyn's father-in-law, Lord Morley, turned to Cromwell – his 'synguler goode frende and olde aqwayntanse' – as a patron and solicited his help in a property dispute with the prior of Norwich cathedral. The suit was successful and he presented Cromwell, a keen hunter, with an appropriate gift in the form of a sleek greyhound. Over the next years, as Morley's position became more precarious in the aftermath of the Boleyn affair, the requests for favours continued and the tokens of appreciation increased in magnitude, culminating in Morley's translation into English for Cromwell's pleasure of the

Plutarchian Life of the Greek king Agesilaus, recently identified as MS 17038C in the National Library of Wales. In the preface, Morley weighed the virtues of the valiant Greek against those of the English king. Understandably, perhaps, he gave Henry a higher ranking in terms of grace and justice, generosity, valour and counsel; what seems preposterous to a modern reader, however, is his concluding point: 'who is more temperat in all thinges, in eting, in drinkyng and in other voluptyose plesurs then oure Henry?' Obviously the book was meant for Henry's eyes as well as those of Cromwell, but, as the learned Tudor historian Sir Geoffrey Elton observed, 'I am sure you had to say these things about the great Henry, and I am reasonably sure that when he read them Cromwell sneered.'

Morley's desire to use Cromwell as a means of access to the king is even more apparent in the copies of Machiaevelli's *Istorie Fiorentine* and *Il Principe* which he asked Cromwell to convey to Henry. Although the books themselves are not known to have survived, the accompanying letter does. In it Morley, like Bardi, turned to Florence and noted the parallels between the revolt of the Florentines against Sixtus IV and Henry's own struggles. He hoped, therefore, that Cromwell would show the 'very words' of the *Istorie Fiorentine* to Henry; in order to make things easier, 'I have notyd it with a hand or with wordes in the marjant to the intent it schuld be in a redynes to youe at all tymes in the redyng'. Morley, it seems, was punctilious in every detail, and the analogy with Bardi's thinking earlier in the decade is a strong one. This is a fine example, too, of the manner in which marginalia were used without compunction as a signalling device in the early modern period.

As Morley realized, Cromwell was acutely aware of the potential of the printed book as an agent of persuasion and at Cromwell's request Morley presented Henry at New Year 1539 with his highly antipapal exposition of Psalm 94 (Ps. 93 in the Vulgate). The book almost immediately found its way into print – it was published by the king's printer, Thomas Berthelet, as *The Exposition and Declaration of the Psalme, Deus ultionum Dominus, made by Syr Henry Parker knight, Lord Morley, dedicated to the Kynges Highnes* – and the Lord Privy Seal, as Cromwell had become in succession to Anne Boleyn's father, must have been the recipient of a copy, now unfortunately lost. In *The Exposition and Declaration* Morley – who was in reality a loyal supporter of the old faith – showed himself positively vehement, not to mention bombastic, in his rejection of the pope:

> For where as unto this presente tyme of your most happy reigne, this youre Empire mooste triumphant, hath ben wrongfully kept, as tributarie unto the Babylonicall seate of the Romyshe byshop, your moste sage and polytike wisedome hath benne suche, that as it maye be well thoughte, by divine inspiration, ye have taken a very kynges harte, whiche seketh, as it ought, to rule, and nat to be ruled. and hath set the Englysshe nation at fredoome and lybertie.

Long after Cromwell's death and once Mary ascended to the throne, Morley provided a gloss to these sentiments, which he no longer endorsed; in the 'Account of the Miracles of the Sacrament', presented to the new queen

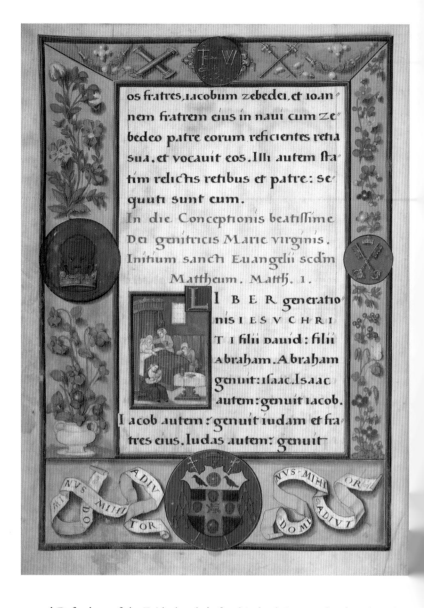

os fratres, iacobum zebedei, et ioan
nem fratrem eius in naui cum ze
bedeo patre eorum reficientes reria
sua, et vocauit eos. Illi autem sta
tim relichs retibus et patre: se
quuti sunt eum.
In die Conceptionis beatissime
Dei genitricis Marie virginis.
Initium sancti Euangelii secdm
Mattheum. Matth. 1.
LIBER generatio
nis IESV CHRI
TI filii Dauid: filii
Abraham. Abraham
genuit: isaac. Isaac
autem: genuit iacob.
Iacob autem: genuit iudam et fra
tres eius. Iudas autem: genuit

78–79. Illumination in Christ
Church 101 is dated to 1528,
but Wolsey's arms in Magdalen
College Lat 223 impale those
of the Sees of York and
Winchester. In Christ Church
101 the monogram TC is used,
whereas in Magdalen College
Lat 223 TW occurs.
The President and Fellows at Magdalen
College, Oxford, MS lat. 223 f. 3v &
Christ Church, Oxford, MS 101, f. 32r

and Defendress of the Faith shortly before his death in 1556, he abominated
the time not so long before when 'this your realme was brought to that sedy-
tion, that first they denyed the head of the Church, the Pope's Holynes, next
wolde have no saintes honored but threwe vile matter at the Crucifyx, and,
adding mischeife to myscheife, denyed the sevyn sacramentes of the
Church'. This kind of sacrilegious behaviour – in which he himself had
indulged – now caused Morley to observe that 'I can thynke noone other but
that the ende of the worlde hastythe apasse accordynge as Christe saide, that
ther shulde cum fals prophettes in the ende of the wourlde that with their
false techynges shulde seduce many'. His volte-face, it should be stated in
fairness, was not necessarily as time-serving as it might appear to modern
eyes, since the events of Edward's reign may well have convinced him that

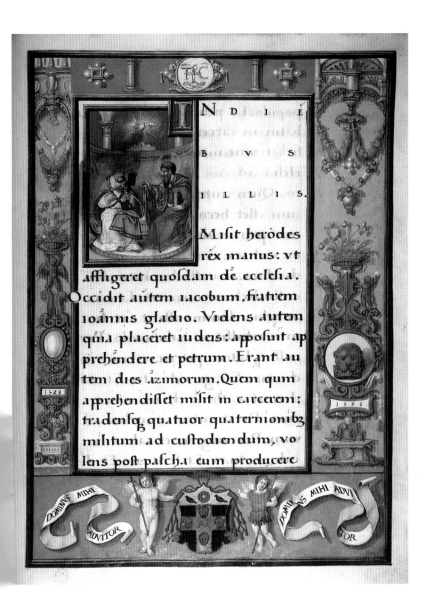

the Roman church could not be abandoned without grave consequences to the Catholic faith. Whatever, else, he certainly was not alone in his shift of ground.

Another member of Cromwell's propaganda team was Sir Richard Morison (*c.*1514–1556), a highly committed reformer whose pamphlets formed a major component of Cromwell's political campaign after the break with Rome. Morison dedicated his *Apomaxis calumniarum* (London, 1537) to Cromwell – it is a learned response, full of quotations from classical literature, to the attack on Henry by the German humanist Johannes Cochlaeus – and the copy which the Protestant reformer John ('Bilious') Bale saw at Westminster in 1548, now lost, may well have derived from Cromwell's library. The presentation copy to Cromwell of Sir Thomas

Elyot's 1538 Dictionary, published by Berthelet, survives; it contains an autograph letter from the author as well as a Westminster inventory number. In the letter Elyot assures Cromwell, a longtime patron, that 'you will be very fond of me because I have kept the laws of friendship'. Dedicated to Henry, the Dictionary was the first Latin–English lexicon to be based on humanist ideals of classical scholarship. According to the preface, Cromwell, Sir Anthony Denny, keeper of Westminster Palace, and the royal librarian William Tyldesley informed the king about the project just before its publication and the latter graciously offered Elyot both advice and access to the royal library. The wealth of material to which he was thus exposed rendered Elyot so dissatisfied with his earlier researches that he had the presses stopped while he carried out revisions and he also added an appendix for the first part of the alphabet which had already been set. Possible flattery aside, such conduct by such a renowned scholar is a strong tribute to the range and diversity of Henry's library during the second half of his reign.

Perhaps the most important book to emerge during Cromwell's ascendency was the Great Bible, published in 1539 – that is in the same year and in the same milieu as Morley's Psalm exposition appeared – and so called because of its size, more than fifteen inches long and more than ten inches broad. At the time of its appearance royal injunctions were issued requiring every parish church to own a copy. As a result there was an immense print run of perhaps twenty thousand copies. This was the first authorized Bible in English – translated, as the title states 'after the veryte of the Hebrue and Greke textes, by ye dylygent studye of dyverse excellent learned men, expert in the forsayde tonges' – and it is a revision and completion by Miles Coverdale of the Matthew Bible of 1537. Cromwell himself, whom Coverdale called the 'causer therof', contributed six hundred marks towards the enterprise. In return for Cromwell's patronage Coverdale caused two copies on 'parchment' to be printed, one for the king and one for Cromwell. These two enormous vellum copies do survive, one at St John's College, Cambridge and one at the National Library of Wales, but it is impossible to determine who received which one. (81) The title page of the Great Bible illustrates vividly the message that Cromwell and the king wished to convey: that Henry is disseminator of the Word of God to his people and supreme head of the English church. The king is thus shown handing out the 'Verbum Dei' to Cranmer and Cromwell, followed respectively by churchmen and nobles. Iconographically the Great Bible was a powerful propaganda tool. (82)

Apart from these few examples, no other books can be linked to Cromwell, which is surprising since he is known to have acquired monastic manuscripts at the Dissolution and he was regularly presented with manuscripts as well as printed books by supplicants. A letter to the Council by his former protégé Ralph Sadler, written on 11 April 1545, long after Cromwell's execution for treason in 1540, may explain what happened. In this letter Sadler stated that he and Cuthbert Tunstall had delivered a calendar of all books, records and letters belonging to Cromwell to the king. Most of these were still at the library at Cromwell's home at Austin Friars:

'Except certain treaties delivered into the treasury of the Exchequer and a few books had into the King's library, all remain in the late lord Crumwell's library in the Augustynes'. Apparently these never were transferred to royal ownership and their ultimate fate is unknown.

One of Henry VIII's favourites – a skilled jouster and gentleman of the Privy Chamber as well as Master of the Horse – Sir Nicholas Carew was described in his youth as 'well-mannered and having the French tongue'. (80) As a result of his supposed involvement in the Exeter conspiracy, when members of the Pole family and others were judicially murdered to eliminate any possible threat to the succession, he was attainted and executed for treason in 1539. His residence, Beddington Place in Surrey – a lovely house where Henry had visited Jane Seymour before they were married – fell to the king along with its contents. At the time of the post-mortem inventory of Henry's goods, twenty-one books, all of which had belonged to Carew, were found among sundry parcels at Beddington. Most were in French and the group showed a strong historical/literary component. Oddly, almost half were copies of the same work, that is Froissart's chronicle: four copies of the first volume, three of the second volume, two of the third and one

80. Painted in armour, Carew is shown holding his lance as a reminder of his prowess in tournament.
In the collection of The Duke of Buccleugh and Queensbury, KT

copy simply described as 'Frosort'. Carew's wife Elizabeth was the niece of Lord Berners, the translator of Froissart. When Berners himself died his goods were seized and an inventory survives: it mentions eighty (unnamed) books, all in French or Latin. Although what subsequently happened to the books was not recorded, a possible recipient would have been Elizabeth Carew, at whose request Berners translated Diego de San Pedro's *Cárcel de amor* as *The Castell of Love*, and who is known to have owned at least one book in her own right, a fifteenth-century copy of John Lydgate's *Fall of Princes*. Alternatively, Berners might have given books to her and her husband during the period between 1526 and 1531 when he left his position as Deputy of Calais and resided in England. Whatever else, Berners must provide the explanation for the dominating presence of Froissart in the Beddington collection.

From the very opening of the debate over the validity of Henry's marriage to Catherine of Aragon, John Fisher, bishop of Rochester, had come down on the queen's side and he wrote extensively on the issue. He was a meticulous examiner of sources and in his unpublished *Breuis apologia seu confutatio* of the government-sponsored *Grauissimae atque exactissimae illustrissimarum totius Italiae et Galliae academiarum censurae* (*The Determinations of the moste famous and excellent uniuersities of Italy and Fraunce, that it is so unlawful for a man to marry his brother's wife and the pope hath no power to dispense therewith* in Thomas Cranmer's translation) he turned to the originals of the patristic

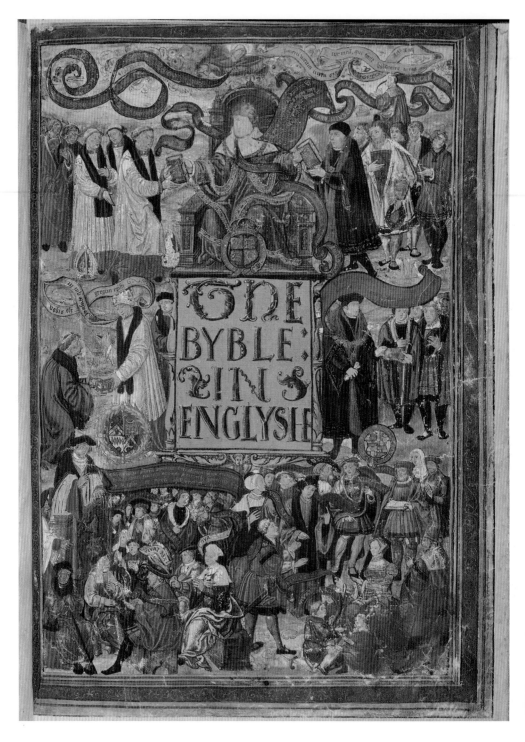

81. The Great Bible stands as a tribute, intellectually and visually, to the defeat of the pope's dominion in England. By permission of the Master and Fellows of St John's College, Cambridge, Bb, title page

82. In the British Library copy of the slightly revised version of the Great Bible, completed after Cromwell's fall and execution (on the right), his image has been replaced with that of an elderly bearded figure; his arms have been gouged off the title page.   The British Library, C.18.d.10, title page

texts cited in the latter and noted misquotations and inaccurate contextual-izations. Fisher was arrested on 6 April 1534 and executed in the spring of 1535. His library, reputedly 'the notablest lybrarye of bookes in all England, two long galleryes full', was housed in his palace at Rochester. Those of his books which were not destroyed after his final arrest (according to the anonymous author of Fisher's life the commissioners 'came to is library of books, which they spoiled in the most pitiful wise, scattering them in such sort as it was lamentable to behold') were almost certainly sequestered, but there are no books in the royal library which show direct evidence of his ownership. In order to refute the position of Henry's supporters in the king's Great Matter, Fisher must have had access to similar sorts of materials as his opponents, and for monastic texts his most obvious source would have been the library at Rochester cathedral priory. As it happens, there are more than one hundred surviving books from the Westminster collection which come from Rochester; no other monastic library was plundered in a similar man-ner – the next largest batch come from St Augustine's Canterbury (almost thirty), followed by St Albans (around twenty), and in both these cases the books dribbled in rather than arriving in a single group. The greatest por-tion of the Rochester group consists of works by the church fathers; this is followed by glossed books of the Bible, including two commentaries on Leviticus, and writings by English historians, such as William of Malmes-bury and Bede. What we have, in fact, is a mirror image of the collection assembled at Westminster by those making a case for the king. Ultimately the evidence is not conclusive, but the most convincing way of accounting for the appearance of this block of books in the royal collection is to assume it came from Fisher. (83)

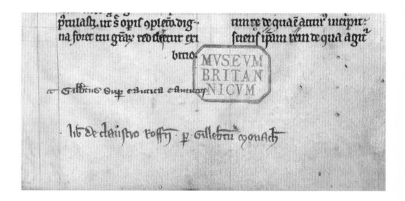

83. This early thirteenth-century copy of Gilbert Foliot's Commentary on the Song of Songs is one of the Rochester books which came to the royal library; it can be identified by the medieval *ex libris* 'Liber de claustro Roffensi per Gillebertum monachum'.
The British Library,
Royal MS 2.E.VII, f. 4r

The monastic component

The Henrician provenance of the Rochester books leads directly to the ques-tion of monastic manuscripts in general and their removal to the royal library during the 1530s. The chief piece of evidence on the topic is a list of almost one hundred manuscripts in Lincolnshire houses, with the heading 'Tabula librorum de historiis antiquitatum ac diuinitate tractancium in librariis et domibus religiosis' ('A list of books treating ancient histories and divinity in libraries and religious houses'). After its compilation the *tabula* was given to a person in authority – some scholars have argued that it was the king himself – who placed a cross beside almost forty titles. These were delivered to the royal collection, where most of them still can be found. (84) One of the codices contains a copy of Ralph of Flaix's commentary on

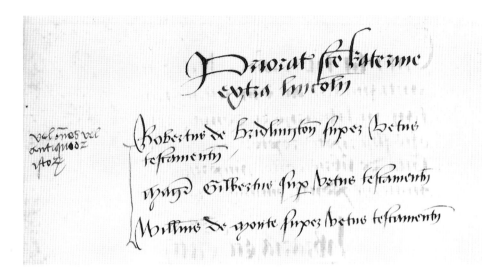

Leviticus, of which Henry got hold of some half dozen copies around 1530; another is a copy from the Augustinian priory at Thornton-on-Humber of the *De gestis pontificum* ('Deeds of the English Bishops') by the brilliant twelfth-century monk and historian William of Malmesbury. (85) The Lincolnshire list is the only document of this type to survive, but it would not have been unique, as references in other state papers indicate. On 27 November 1530, for example, an inventory of books from Reading Abbey was sent to Hampton Court. Even if the inventory itself is no longer extant, we can deduce that it was examined and marked up precisely in the manner of the Lincolnshire list, since an abbey servant was paid forty shillings on 29 November – just two days later – for delivering books to Hampton Court. On 27 January 1531 a servant of the abbot of Ramsey got twenty shillings for bringing books to Westminster, and in February books arrived from Sempringham and Gloucester, followed by Spalding, Evesham and Worcester.

This early phase of monastic acquisition was, it is clear, a direct result of Henry's attempt to rid himself of Catherine of Aragon, a concern which became irrelevant in 1533 when he took matters into his own hands and married Anne Boleyn without having obtained the requisite annulment. This move involved a challenging of the pope's authority and it led inevitably to the assertion for England of both independence from Rome and imperial status. The wording of the Preamble of the Act in Restraint of Appeals of April 1533 is revealing in its statement that: 'by divers sundry

84. Beside the list of three books from the Gilbertine priory of St Catherine the annotator has written 'uel omnes uel antiquior istorum' ('either all of them or the older').
The British Library,
Royal MS Appendix 69, f. 2v

old authentic histories and chronicles it is manifestly declared and expressed that this realm of England is an empire, and so hath been accepted in the world, governed by one supreme head and king having the dignity and royal estate of the imperial crown of the same'. The 1533 act was followed by the Act of Supremacy of 1534, where, once again, 'divers sundry old authentic histories' were cited. By the end of 1534, then, Henry had become supreme head of the church under God: henceforth the pope's authority in England was null and void. At this point, it became illegal even to call him pope and the word was routinely either excised from ancient writings or substituted with 'bishop of Rome'. Gone was the papal tiara, gone was Peter's Pence, gone were all the complications of international canon law.

On 21 January 1535, just two months after Parliament acknowledged Henry as supreme head of the church in England, Thomas Cromwell was appointed vicegerent for the purpose of undertaking a general ecclesiastical visitation of England and Wales. One of the primary functions of the visitation was to ensure acceptance of the supremacy, but Cromwell also concerned himself with books. From Bath, he obtained two manuscripts, the first dispatched by one of the official visitors, the notoriously heavy-handed and hard-hearted Richard Layton, who stated: 'Ye shalle receve a bowke of our lades miracles well able to mache the *Canterberies Tailles*. Such a bowke of dremes as ye never sawe wich I fownde in the librarie.' The second, sent to Cromwell on 25 September 1535 by the prior, came as the result of the perusal of the library by the royal librarian: 'I have send your maister-shipp hereyn an old boke *Opera Anselmi* which one William Tildysleye after scrutinye made here in my libarye willed me to send unto youe by the kynge ys grace and commawndment.' Anselm, prior of Bec and later archbishop of Canterbury (d. 1109), is remembered nowadays primarily for his onto-logical proof of the existence of God, but what must have caught Tyldesley's eye was Anselm's dispute with William II over the extent of the king's right to interfere in Church matters.

Later in same year the prior of Christ Church, Twinham, in Hamp-shire, wrote to Cromwell stating: 'I send you Beda *De ecclesiastica historia*, and another chronicle, whose author I do not know, wherein also another treatise *De gestis pontificum Anglorum*. The other book which you desire, *De gestis Anglorum*, cannot yet be found; but as soon as I may have him, if he be within our house, I will send him without delay.' This letter is evidence of a calculated acquisition policy on Cromwell's part, books carefully chosen after preliminary researches by advance scouts. As a result of the haul from Lincolnshire, the royal library already possessed a copy of William of Malmesbury's *De gestis pontificum*; Cromwell's advisors must have hoped that further anti-papal, pro-English precedents could be found in William's *Gesta regum Anglorum* ('History of the English Kings') as well as in Bede's comprehensive ecclesiastical history of the early English church.

The abbot of Winchcombe delivered 'certain books' to Cromwell. A turncoat member of the same community, John Horwood (or in religion Placett), 'sowzht mony wolde bokys and ragyde pawmphylions de Purgato-rio pro et contra' for Cromwell, as well as a letter sent to Pope John against

85. This signalling of the discussion of consanguinity in marriage in William's *De gestis pontificum* pertains to Henry's own marital troubles at the period.
The British Library, Harley MS 2, f. 130r

pride and covetousness, a papistical book, a leaf of absolution and other offending works. The 1535 visitations continued the earlier trend, therefore, of appropriating books which might provide evidence against recalcitrant religious, or might be cited in the context of the supremacy and the overthrow of papal jurisdiction.

Basing himself on the evidence of the 1535 visitations, Cromwell presented a bill in February 1536 for the suppression of all religious houses with an annual income of less than £200, and this became law in March. (In the 1520s the hopeful Boleyn client Simon Fish had already argued that the parasitical clergy should be deprived of their ill-gotten gains and in any case the primary function of monasteries as purgatorial institutions, that is as places which served to offer prayers for the souls of their founders and patrons, had fallen out of fashion even before Henry's break with Rome.) The subsequent failure of the Pilgrimage of Grace – a popular uprising which attempted to salvage English monastic life – was the cause for further suppressions. Finally, in 1539 there was a second Act of Dissolution, primarily a recognition of a *fait accompli* as a result of voluntary suppressions, but also a signal for the dismemberment of the few establishments remaining. This was sometimes accompanied, as at Glastonbury, by the execution of the abbot and the most recalcitrant monks. The lands and valuables of the dissolved houses were handed over to the king, the process handled by the Court of Augmentations. The break with Rome now fully accomplished, there was no longer any concerted effort to salvage books for the royal collection. Although some were taken away by departing religious, some sold, and some rescued by the monastic visitors and interested antiquaries, manuscripts were not usually highly valued and in general John Bale's analysis in *The Laboryouse Journey & serche of Johan Leylande for Englandes Antiquitees* of the post-dissolution situation can be taken as accurate:

> A great nombre of them which purchased those superstycyouse mansyons reserved of those lyrarye bokes, some to serve theyr jakes, some to scoure theyr candelstyckes, & some to rubbe their bootes. Some they solde to the grossers and sope sellers, & some they sent over see to the bokebynders, not in small nombre, but at tymes whole shyppes full, to the wonderynge of the foren nacyons.

The reference to 'jakes' may be a rhetorical one, but there is firm evidence that manuscripts were cut up and used by bookbinders and grocers: a practice that carried on well into the seventeenth century when, for example, a particularly important medieval manuscript from Glastonbury was salvaged after an Oxford student sent out for tobacco and found leaves from it wrapping his purchase.

No national archive as such was established in Henry's reign, in spite of John Leland's valiant attempts, and the relatively modest monastic component of the Henrician library came into being as a result of the concerns of 1527 to 1535 and perhaps shortly afterwards (i.e. when the question of General Councils was dominating Henry's thinking). Most of the books entering the royal collection in the late 1530s consisted of contemporary texts rather than monastic strays and reflect the move in the direction of reform, as alliances were being established which ultimately would lead to the marriage with Anne of Cleves in 1540. After the failure of the marriage and Cromwell's resulting execution no coherent acquisitions policy can be detected.

John Leland's role

The tradition that the title of *antiquarius* adopted by John Leland had any kind of official status is entirely without substance. (86) Nor is there any evidence that he was ever appointed special librarian to the king in parallel with the creation of the position of Master of the King's Library in France for Guillaume Budé in 1522. According to Leland's own testimony, never-theless, he acted 'by the authoryte of your moste gracyouse commyssion, in the .xxxv. [in error for .xxv., i.e. 1533] yeare of your prosperouse reygne, to peruse and dylygentlye to searche all the lybraryes of monasteryes and collegies of thys your noble realme'. Elsewhere in his writings he referred to some sort of letter ('diploma') from the king, which was very effective even with the most recalcitrant monastic officials. At the Cistercian house at Jervaulx, for example, Leland complacently observed that 'once the abbot had read the king's letter he showed me every kindness and took me immediately into his library.'

Leland began touring monastic houses almost immediately after Anne Boleyn's coronation at the end of May 1533, and his surviving booklists were usually compiled before the dissolutions of the houses which he visited. His brief sketches of the monastic libraries, found in his uncompleted bio-bibliography of British authors, *De uiris illustribus*, suggest widely differing conditions from house to house and order to order. For the most part, the Benedictines were singled out for praise and Leland was lyrical in his evocation of the well-stocked library at Glastonbury:

86. No contemporary likeness of Leland survives: this lost bust, known only from a woodcut and completely imaginary in its characterization, was executed by Louis François Roubiliac for the library at All Soul's College Oxford in the mid-eighteenth century.
John Leland (from frontispiece to William Huddesford's *Life of John Leland*).
British Library, 674.f.21

> A few years ago I was in Glastonbury, Somerset, where the oldest and the most famous abbey of our whole island is found. Wearied by the long labours of research I was refreshing my spirits by the kindness of Richard Whiting, abbot of the place, until a certain enthusiasm for reading and learning should inflame me afresh. This enthusiasm came sooner than I had expected, and so I betook myself at once to the library (which is not open to all comers) in order to turn over the relics of venerable antiquity, of which the number there is not easily matched anywhere else in Britain. Indeed, I had hardly crossed the threshold when the mere sight of the ancient books left me awestruck, stupefied in fact, and because of this I stood hesitating a little while. Then, having saluted the *genius loci*, I spent some days searching through all the bookcases with the greatest curiosity.

In a passage judiciously deleted from the final version of the text he describes the abbot as 'homine sane candidissimo, ac amico singulari meo' ('a truly splendid man, and a very close friend of mine').

Not all collections were as well maintained as this and Leland's search for writings by Roger Bacon was frustrating. Although Bacon's writings

> were once disseminated in many copies and kept religiously in libraries all over Britain, now, I am ashamed to say, some of them have been removed from their bookcases and carried off by theft through their guardians' negligence; others have become mutilated, with quires torn out here and there; in fact, they appear so seldom that it would be easier for to collect the Sybilline leaves than the names of the books which he wrote.

Bacon was a Franciscan and Leland's strongest disapproval was directed towards the keepers of the library of the Oxford Franciscans. When he asked to see the library:

> several asses gawped at me, braying that hardly any mortal man was allowed to approach such a holy precinct and sanctuary to see the mysteries, except the Warden – for so they call their head – and the bachelors of his sacred College. But I pressed them and, armed with the king's letter, more or less forced them to open up their shrines. At last one of the senior donkeys, with much humming and hawing, reluctantly unlocked the doors. Good God! What did I find there? Nothing but dust, cobwebs, bookworms, cockroaches, in short filth and destitution. I did find some books, but I should not willingly have paid threepence for them. So, searching for diamonds I found nothing but cinders.

The mendicant orders as a whole fared badly in Leland's account and he also dismissed 'the dust of the Dominican library in Oxford'. In part, his rhetoric reflects the general unpopularity of the friars in the mid-1530s, but there was, as other evidence suggests, some truth in his assertions.

To judge by his writings, it was relatively unusual for Leland to remove materials from the monasteries while they were still functioning, either for his personal collection or for the royal library. In some instances, however, he did gather up books which seemed unusual or germane to royal concerns: a copy of Bede's commentary on Ezra and Nehemiah from Cirencester, say, or Claudius Taurinensis's commentary on Matthew from Lanthony. From Malmesbury, which he visited during an abbatial vacancy, several manuscripts migrated into his own collection, including a very early and now lost manuscript of the writings of Tertullian, the first of the church fathers to write in Latin. He was particularly keen for Henry to take possession of manuscripts formerly owned by King Athelstan (d. 939), perhaps because Athelstan claimed kingship of the English and lordship over all of Albion (i.e. Scotland and Wales) as well. At Bath Priory Leland found a copy of the *Acts of the Council of Constantinople* (680) written on the continent towards the end of the ninth century and given to the monks by Athelstan; he rescued this gem for the king after having entered liminary verses in it:

> Athelstan was the principal agent of my preservation;
> I knew his library well.
> After his death, for six hundred years and more
> I lay hidden, filthy in dust and mould.
> At last the concern of great Henry recalled me
> To the light of day, and restored me to a worthy place.

The verses are no longer in the book – perhaps they were on a detached flyleaf – but they do occur in another of Athelstan's books, which was at St Augustine's Canterbury before Leland transferred it 'to the palace library of that most illustrious prince Henry VIII.' (87)

After the Dissolution Leland continued to gather up materials for the king and for himself too. In some cases old books were left behind in the

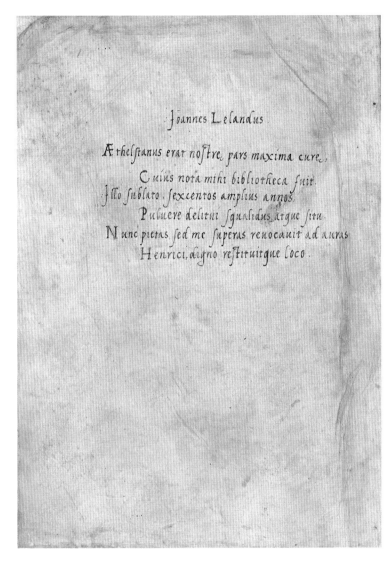

·Joannes Lelandus.

Æthelstanus erat nostre pars maxima cure,
  Cuius nota mihi bibliotheca fuit.
Illo sublato, sexcentos amplius annos,
  Puluere delitui squalidus atque situ.
Nunc pietas sed me superas renocauit ad auras
  Henrici, digno restituitque loco.

87. Leland's verses are entered
in a tenth-century copy of the
Gospels, which also contains
a note in an eleventh-century
hand stating that the book was
given by Athelstan himself
to St Augustine's.
The British Library,
Royal MS I.A. XVIII, f. 2v

ruined buildings and in others Leland made contact with former religious, as at Sherborne, from whom he appropriated books. His concerns were more general, more historical and patriotic, than those of the earlier monastic visitors — whose efforts Archbishop Matthew Parker would describe later in the century as having been undertaken 'leuiter et perfunctorie' (quickly and in a perfunctory manner) — and his contribution to the shape of the royal library and to the recovery of the British past is perhaps more crucial than has been generally recognized. As he himself put it in his *New Year's Gift*, his 'perusal' and 'searching out' of *all* the monastic libraries in the kingdom ultimately led to the bringing 'out of deadly darkenesse to lyvely light' the 'monumentes of auncyent wryters', to be deposited in 'the most magnifcent libraryes of your royall palaces.'

During the period Henry was composing his *Assertio septem sacramentorum*, his secretary Richard Pace came into his presence and discovered him reading a book written by his 'bête noir', Martin Luther, which had been delivered by Wolsey, the latter acting in his role as senior research assistant. By Pace's account, Henry dipped into controversial writings of this nature; sometimes he made marginal annotations, but like a modern administrator – or talk-show presenter – he normally sent the book out to a team of experts and asked them to provide a 'gist' for him. In the late 1520s and early 1530s, when Henry was concerned with the examination of 'old authentic histories and chronicles' and what they might be made to reveal in the context of his matrimonial troubles, various individuals presented him with relevant materials. A fourteenth-century copy of the world chronicle of William of Nangis, monk of St Denis (d. 1300) formerly owned by Thomas Howard, duke of Norfolk (1524–54) came to Henry about this time. Clearly Henry was pleased to receive it and he consulted it carefully; the manuscript has a number of marginal notes in his hand, many relating to the authority of the pope and questions of consanguinity. (88) When a

88. By this passage in Nangis's chronicle Henry has written in his highly characteristic and somewhat old-fashioned script, 'prima destructio ydolum in Anglia' ('the first destruction of idols in England').
The British Library,
Royal MS 13.E. IV, f. 290v

book interested him, Henry was a compulsive annotater, and his copies of Erasmus's works are deeply scored (usually positively), as are his copies of Luther (negatively). Henry actively engaged with texts which furthered his own desires or whims at any given time; at the end of his life, for example, he found the admonition in verse 10 of Psalm 62 that we should 'Truste not in ryches gotten wyth wronge and forse' to be 'pulchra doctrina' ('a fine teaching').

As we have seen, Henry's agents scoured Europe to find ancient documents to support his rejection of his marriage to his brother's widow: these researches culminated in the impressive sounding *Grauissimae atque exactissimae illustrissimarum totius Italiae et Galliae academiarum censurae*. Although the *Censurae* cited councils of the church, the fathers and so forth, not all scholars were convinced by the evidence: amongst others, one of Catherine of Aragon's chaplains, Thomas Abell, wrote his *Inuicta ueritas* ('Unconquered Truth') in response. In this treatise, published in 1532, Abell argued vigorously against the 'official' position of the Henrician regime. The king's copy of the *Inuicta ueritas* is now found at Lambeth Palace. Henry read the text carefully and marked off irritating passages; challenging, for example, Abell's interpretation of the laws of consanguinity, which was at the heart of the annulment question, with a resounding 'yt ys false'. (89) As a result of his efforts, poor

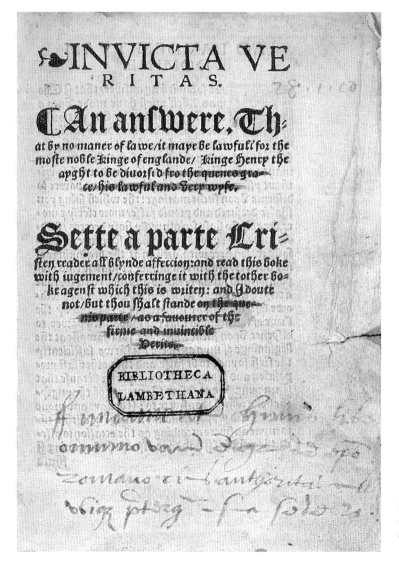

89. On the title page of Abell's *Invicta ueritas* is scribbled: 'Fundamentum hujus libri vanum est' ('The basic premise of this book is worthless'). Lambeth Palace Library, 1532.4.01, title page

Abell found himself in the Tower for a time; in the later Cromwellian purge of 1540, he fared even worse: convicted of high treason he was hanged, drawn and quartered at Smithfield.

Henry's matrimonial trials continued in one form or another long after he extricated himself from his first marriage and one can only guess at his thoughts when he noted 'Ergo nec in nobis' ('Therefore neither in ours')

aliquid naturale potest intelligi dupliciter vel a natura sola sine actu ani
me ut motus lapidis et tale nõ pt assuefieri in cõtrariũ vel a natura cũ ac
tu anime et tale pt assuefieri in cõtrariũ Vnde aues docentur hoim voces
articulatas formare.

D scdm sic pcedit videtur eñ cp aliqñ auctoritate humana fuit dispẽ
satũ ples vxores habere cp in illis que nõ sũt cõtra naturã nec ptra
mores nec contra dei pcepta auctoritate humana dispẽsari potest ß dicit
glosa aug. Gen. xxix cp plicas vxorũ iacob nõ fuit cõtra naturã nec cõtra
mores nec cõtra dei pcepta. ergo in hoc auctoritate hũana dispẽsatũ fuit.

P Amb dicit cp Abraham qñ plures vxores habuit nõ cõmisit aliquid
cõtra legem ß puenit legem. In omni aut eo cp nõ est cõtra legẽ diuinam
dispẽsari pt auctoritate humana P dispẽsatio cadit sup eo cp nõ est cõ
tra legẽ nature ß pseruatio speciei humane quã natũ oim animaliũ dic
tat in suo gñe seruat Vet certi cp fieri p pluralitate vxorũ cp aliter solũ er
go auctoritate humana in hoc cadit dispẽsatio. In cõtrariũ ẽ cp hũana
auctoritas nõ se extẽdit dispẽsare in eo cp est ptra naturã et cõtra mores
Sz glosa Gen. iiij dicit cp pmus ptra naturã et mores cõmittẽs adulteri
um fuit Lamech qui accepit duas vxores. R. Dicẽdũ cp scdm aug. duo
pcipue ostendũt solũ dei auctoritate dispẽsatũ esse in pluritate vxorũ. Pri
mũ est diuini cultus ampliatio. Scdm est sanctorũ patz deuotio. In suc
cessione nãqz sanguinis sicut dicit aug. erat successio religionis in qñ cole
bat deus Vnde cp gẽtis fideliũ distincte ab infidelibz pm9 pater fuit abra
hã. Ideo in eo pmo factũ est puilegiũ diuine dispẽsacõnis de plibz haben
dis vxoribz et sic successiue oibz posteris ei9 in qbz fuit eade causa ppaga
tionis fidelis ppli. Secũdo hoc ostendit sanctoz patz deuotio Cõtrahebãt
eñ ßm Aug. sancti patres cũ pluribz vxoribz nõ ducti libidine ß ducti pi
etate cp vtebant piugibz pluribz castius qñ nũc vna quilibz istoz in qui
bus videmus cp ßm veritate concedit apostol9 qui attestat eoz meritũ ait
eñ cp sicut nõ fuit impar meritũ patientie in Petro qñ passus est a in Joh
qui passus nõ est. sic ñ fuit impar meritũ continẽtie in Johe qñ nullas exp
tus est nuptias et in abrahã qñ filios gñauit. nã illius celibatus et istius
cõnubiũ p tepoz distributione xpo militauerut. Quãuis eñ castitas celi
bũ melioz sit qm castitas nuptiarũ. abraham tñ ambas habuit vnã i ha
bitu a vnã sola in vsu. Ad primũ ergo est dicendũ cp plures vxores ha
bere nõ fuit cõtra naturã in antiqs partibz cp nõ fuit ppter affectũ libidi
nosuz ß officiosũ. vnde nõ erat contra legẽ nature exquo sciebãt inẽna in
spiracõne et angelica reuelacõne ipm deũ hoc velle. Quãuis eñ ratio na
turalis absolute dictet nõ esse accipiẽdã rem alienã dño rei inuito cõditio
nalitet est pt bltate pcedus puta vllo velẽ Exquo ergo simili pacteo
sciebant deũ

beside Augustinus de Ancona's comment in his *Summa de potestate ecclesias-tica* ('Compendium concerning Ecclesiastical Power') published in Cologne in 1475: 'Ad primum ergo est dicendum quod plures uxores habere non fuit contra naturam in antiquis patribus &c' ('First, therefore, it must be said that to have several wives was not against nature in the ancient fathers'). (90)

Although his travelling coffers contained spectacles, Henry did little reading himself as he got older and there are fewer annotations. Writing in 1537 to the Strasbourg reformer Wolfgang Capito, who had sent Henry a copy of his recently completed *Responsio de missa, matrimonio et iure magistratus in religionem*, Cranmer explained that

> the king commonly hands over books of this kind which he has not the patience to read himself to one of his lords in waiting for perusal, from whom he afterwards learns the contents. He then gives them to someone else of an opposite way of thinking. After hearing all their criticisms he declares his own judgment. This I understand he has done with your book, and while much pleased with many things, dis-approves of some – I suspect the statements about the Mass.

In this case the pros did indeed outweigh the cons, in spite of Henry's unalter-able belief in the Real Presence, and Henry rewarded Capito with a hundred crowns. It was an impressive gesture, especially in the context of Capito's relatively radical text, and he must have been highly gratified. Capito was also lucky to have a reliable agent in his dealings with Henry. When in 1542 the Italian satirist Pietro Aretino asked Edmund Harvel, the English ambassador to Venice, to send Henry VIII a copy of the book he had lately dedicated to Henry, the king passed a reward on to Harvel, but as late as 1547 it had not got to Aretino.

At Henry's own command, the royal printer Thomas Berthelet pub-lished in 1537 *The Institution of a Christen man*, popularly known as the 'Bishops' Book', in which the bishops were 'to set forth a plain and sincere doctrine, concerning the whole sum of all those things which appertain unto the profession of a christian man'. Although it did still uphold the doctrine of transsubstantiation, this work moved the English church strongly in the direction of reform; by renumbering the ten commandments, for example, it created a separate commandment prohibiting use of images, which justified a policy which would later become such a destructive part of the Reformation, many of the statues as well as stained glass of the medieval church being broken to pieces by the iconoclasts. Henry was not entirely sat-isfied with the book, however, and in one of his copies there are marginalia as well as some sixty-three added leaves containing draft corrections for cir-culation to the bishops. Another copy, now in the Bodleian Library, has notes by Henry as well as four longer annotations by Cranmer, who was in reality the chief redactor of the work. (92) In his annotations Henry, who was most anxious that faith should not be separated from hope and charity, indicated his disapproval of the apparent drift towards solifidianism among the more evangelical of his clergy; good works were, in his opinion,

90. *Opposite* Apart from entering marginalia Henry marked up the index of Ancona's *Summa de potestate* for future consultation.
The British Library, IB 3131, f. 193v

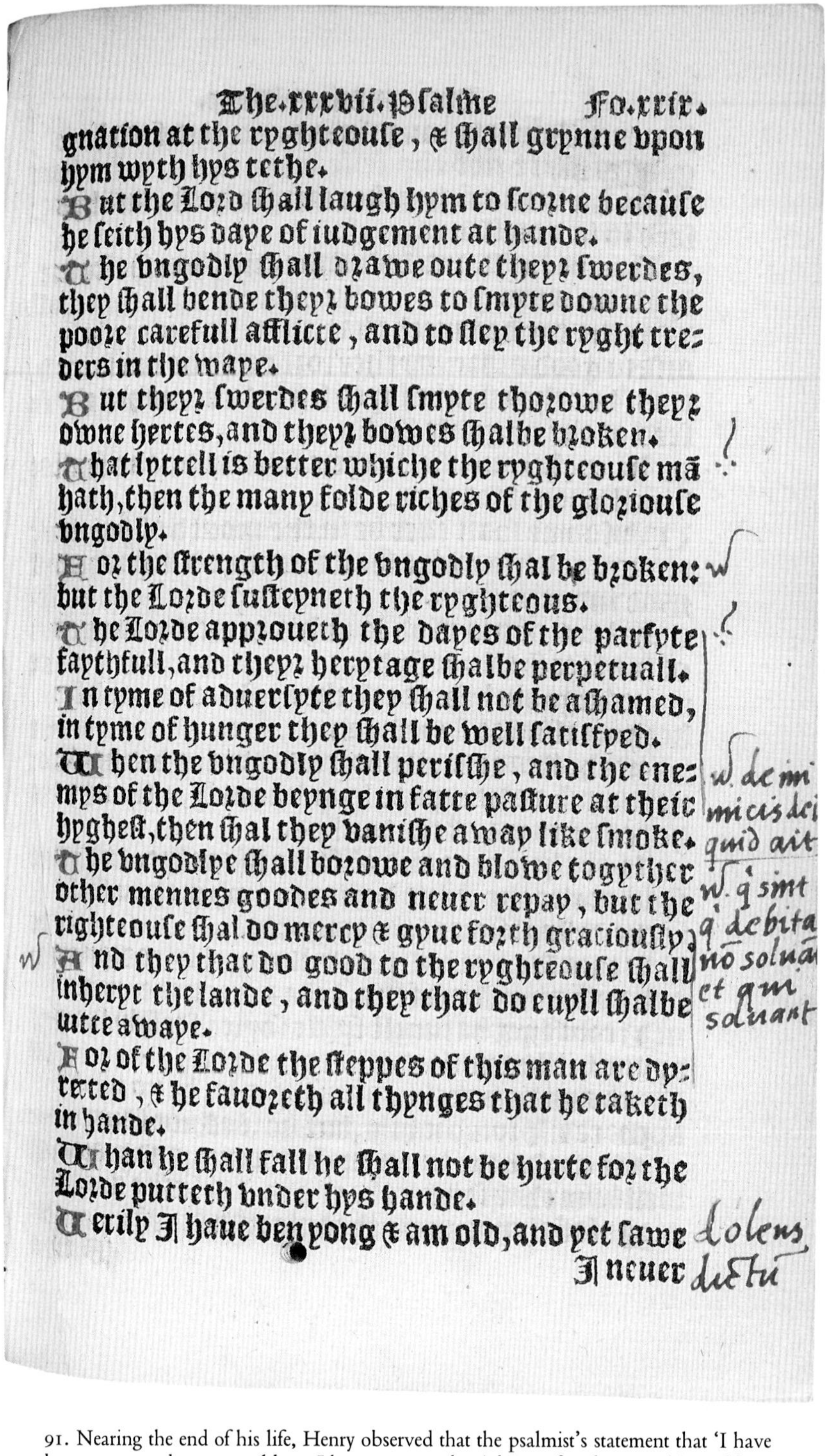
The.xxxvii.Psalme Fo.xxix.

gnation at the ryghteouse, & shall grynne vpon
hym wyth hys tethe.
But the Lord shall laugh hym to scorne because
he seith hys daye of iudgement at hande.
The vngodly shall drawe oute theyr swerdes,
they shall bende theyr bowes to smyte downe the
poore carefull afflicte, and to sley the ryght tre=
ders in the waye.
But theyr swerdes shall smyte thorowe theyr
owne hertes, and theyr bowes shalbe broken.
That lyttell is better whiche the ryghteouse mā
hath, then the many folde riches of the gloriouse
vngodly.
For the strength of the vngodly shal be broken:
but the Lorde susteyneth the ryghteous.
The Lorde approueth the dayes of the parfyte
faythfull, and theyr herytage shalbe perpetuall.
In tyme of aduersyte they shall not be ashamed,
in tyme of hunger they shall be well satisfyed.
When the vngodly shall perische, and the ene=
mys of the Lorde beynge in fatte pasture at their
hyghest, then shal they vanische away like smoke.
The vngodlye shall borowe and blowe togyther
other mennes goodes and neuer repay, but the
righteouse shal do mercy & gyue forth graciously.
And they that do good to the ryghteouse shall
inheryt the lande, and they that do euyll shalbe
utte awaye.
For of the Lorde the steppes of this man are dy=
rected, & he fauoreth all thynges that he taketh
in hande.
Whan he shall fall he shall not be hurte for the
Lorde putteth vnder hys hande.
Verily I haue ben yong & am old, and yet sawe
I neuer

91. Nearing the end of his life, Henry observed that the psalmist's statement that 'I have been young and now am old; yet I have not seen the righteous forsaken, nor his seed begging bread' (Ps. 38:25) was a sad saying (*dolens dictum*). The British Library, C.25.b.4, sig. xxix

as necessary as faith alone. Ultimately, Henry's revisions led to the publication in 1543 of the more conservative 'King's Book'. Whether or not he was
really the author of the treatise, or the degree to which his personal interven-
tions shaped it, may be disputed, but whatever else his well-thumbed and

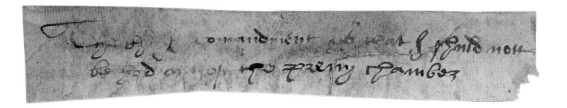

marked-up copies of its predecessor do establish that he kept a close personal
eye on the ecclesiastical policies set out in official publications and show that
his was the final say in doctrinal matters – as he would no doubt have considered fitting and proper for the Defender of the Faith.

92. There is a forceful note at the
front and back of this copy of the
'Bishops' Book': 'The kyngs
comandment ys that I shuld
nott be had out of the prevy
chamber'.
Bodleian Library, Oxford,
Bodl. 4o Rawlinson 245, pasted-in sheet

During the crisis precipitated by the discovery of the adultery of his fifth
wife, Catherine Howard, Henry annotated his copy of the books of
Solomon in the translation by Miles Coverdale. In his marginalia, probably
all made in one sitting, he was particularly attentive to passages relating to
salvation and judgement, kingship, wisdom, riches and marriage. In the
context of his recent experiences it is not surprising that he observed 'nota
bene' beside Proverbs 5:3-12: 'For the lyppes of an harlot are a droppynge
hony combe, and hyr throte is softer then oyle. But at the last she is as bytter
as wormewode, and as sharpe as a two edged sweard...' The annotated
Bokes of Salomon has been bound together with a copy of the psalter in the
English translation of George Joye – whose earlier translation of Proverbs
introduced the expression 'Pride goeth before a fall' into the English language. In the psalter there are also a series of notes; these have been entered
by a professional scribe, who copied them from Henry's own marginalia in
the psalter manuscript produced by Jean Maillart. (91) It is significant that
Henry himself worked from the Latin version and that it was only afterwards that the notes found their way into an English translation. Henry
would have been more familiar with the Latin than the English: conservative
in religion until the end of his life, he also might have felt a residual distrust
of the newly introduced English text.

Not all Henry's annotations concerned political or religious matters and
in an early sixteenth-century Book of Hours illuminated by Flemish artists
there are a pair of notes, perhaps entered as the manuscript was passed clan-
destinely back and forth between Henry and the then woman of his desires,
Anne Boleyn. Henry wrote (in French): 'If you remember me according to
my love in your prayers I shall scarcely be forgotten, since I am your Henry
Rex for ever.' Anne replied (in doggerel English verse): 'Be daly prove you
shall me fynde / To be to you bothe lovynge and kynde.' (93–94)

93 *above* and 94 *opposite*. Both notes relate to the miniature under which they find themselves: The lovesick Henry compared himself to the man of sorrows and chose that image for his lament; and the ever-coy Anne turned to the Annunciation – one must assume, however, that she did not see Henry as the holy spirit descending like a dove. The British Library, King's MS 9, f. 66v; 231v

Three of Henry's wives were learned in their own right and possessed substantial collections of books. It is generally assumed that the first (Catherine
of Aragon) was intellectual and pious – she arrived in England after having
been educated in the sophisticated humanist court of Spain – and that the
last (Catherine Parr) was equally scholarly – after all, she was a writer of
reformist devotional books as well as a peace-maker within the troubled
royal family. About the second wife, Anne Boleyn, there has been more
controversy and she has been characterized either as a committed evangelical
or a fashion-conscious self-server. Most of the accepted generalizations about
these women can be confirmed by an examination of their books, or even
books associated with them through decoration and symbolism, but there are
more subtle points to be made as well. There is less evidence about the other
three wives. In the case of Jane Seymour the literary remains are minimal: the
initials H & I were found on a clasp of an unidentified book among the
queen's coffers after Henry's death, and a book formerly owned by Jane was
given to Catherine Howard by Henry in 1540. An illuminated Book of
Hours, printed in Germany c.1533 and now in the Folger Shakespeare
Library in Washington, D.C., contains a dedication to Henry from Anne
of Cleves; that she signs herself 'Anne the dowther off Cleves' must indicate that the book came after the dissolution of her marriage, when Henry
viewed her as his dear sister rather than devoted wife. Books associated with
Catherine Howard may indicate that she, unlike the others, did value books
for their covers alone, regarding them primarily as decorative objects.

When the Spanish entourage departed after Catherine's marriage to Prince Arthur in 1501, Catherine was overcome by homesickness and melancholy. As an antidote, her new father-in-law 'curtesly lete desire and calle unto him the Princes and her ladies with dyvers ladies of Englond and brought them to a lybrary of is, wherin he shewed unto her many goodly pleasaunt bokes of werkes full delitfull, sage, mery, and also right cunnyng, bothe in Laten and in Englishe'. Henry VII was inordinately proud of his library at Richmond Palace: this description indicates that it was multilingual and contained considerably more than the French manuscripts listed by Palamède Gontier during his 1535 visit.

It is natural that her father-in-law would show Catherine books in Latin as well as English – her English was rudimentary at this stage and her French somewhat laboured, but she was deeply familiar with classical literature as a result of the highly sophisticated tuition provided by her mother Isabella of Castile. Isabella had engaged as tutor to her children Pietro Martire d'Anghierra – whose account of Columbus's journey to the New World, *De orbe nouo*, later came to Henry VIII's collection – and Martire would one day vaunt: 'I was the literary foster-father of almost all the princes, and of all the princesses of Spain.' It was this humanist regime of learning – provided for *both* the princes and princesses – that Catherine would pass on to her daughter Mary, who became a skilled Latinist in her own right. (95)

Towards the end of her life, when Wolsey came to plead with her after her brilliant performance and dramatic departure from the legatine trial of 1529, which challenged the validity of her marriage, Catherine shrewdly insisted that the conversation be conducted in English – 'although I understand Latin' – because she wanted her ladies to hear just what the cardinal had to say. When Catherine first arrived in England, however, Henry VII

95. This lavishly produced Book of Hours which belonged to a lady at court contains a translation from Latin by Mary at the age of eleven of 'The prayor of Saynt Thomas of Aquune'. Note that 'Prynses' and 'Quene Kateryne hys wyfe' have later been expunged from the rubric.
The British Library,
Add. MS 17012, f. 192v

used books to introduce her to the language and culture of her 'brave new world' – that is the milieu to which he expected her to adapt herself. Finally, Henry VII's gesture reminds us that he was a shrewd judge of character and knew what would appeal. On this particular occasion, as it happens, he also had a second card up his sleeve and brought along rings and jewellery in case the intellectual interests of Catherine's attendants, if not the princess herself, began to flag during the course of the tour.

Some thirty years later, in 1533, fortune's wheel having descended, dreams shattered and with only the sense of her God-imposed duty to maintain her, Catherine was banished from court to Buckden Palace in Cambridgeshire, chief residence of the bishops of Lincoln. One of the ways her husband sought to bring her to heel was by denying her access to her beloved daughter Mary. Just before she was removed the following year from Buckden to Kimbolton Castle, even more dreary as far as she was concerned, Catherine wrote a long letter to Mary, seeking to fortify her for what was to come for both of them. As spiritual consolation she sent 'two books in *Latin*; one shall be *De uita Christi* with a declaration of the Gospels, and the other the Epistles of St Jerome that he did write to Paula and Eustochium, and in them I trust you shall find good things'. The first of these is Ludolph of Saxony's *Vita Christi*, which was one of the most popular works of devotion during the fourteenth and fifteenth centuries and was also frequently printed in the sixteenth century. At Lambeth Palace there is a copy of the Paris edition of 1534, which belonged to Mary when she was queen (1553–58). It would be touching to think this was the very book sent to her by her mother and retained ever afterwards, a consolation in the

96. Ludolph of Saxony, *Vita Christi* (Paris: Claude Chevallon 1534). This copy was bound by the King Edward and Queen Mary Binder after Mary came to the throne.
Lambeth Palace Library, **F298(L8), cover

time of her greatest adversity, and a joy in her later triumphs, although more prosaically it is probably another copy given her in 1557 by John Cawood, the Queen's Printer: 'a book in laten entitled uita christi and a little boke of exhortation to young men.' (96)

Up to the mid-1520s, when it became clear that Catherine was not going to produce healthy sons, her marriage – politically motivated though it may have been – was seen as an ideal one and was held up as a model to be emulated, Erasmus asking Henry himself in 1519: 'What family of citizens offers so clear an example of strict and harmonious wedlock? Where could one find a wife more keen to equal her admirable spouse?' Indeed, the Dutch humanist waxed lyrical about the queen's learning, observing with pleasure in a letter of 26 July 1518 to his old friend Paolo Bombace that: 'The queen is astonishingly well read, far beyond what would be surprising in a woman, and as admirable for piety as she is for learning.' In the same year he exlained to Johannes Fabri, vicar-general of the bishop of Constance, that 'The king himself is a most promising student of philosophy. The queen loves good literature, which she has studied with success since childhood. Who would not wish to pass his life in such a court?' Although no books with Catherine's

97. *Below* This miniature of Henry VIII attributed to Lucas Horenbout is dated between June 1525 and June 1527. There is a knotted HK (for Henry and Katherine) in the border above and below the actual portrait: the same monogram appears in books they owned together.
Fitzwilliam Museum, Cambridge

98. *Left* Parallel to the celebration of red and white roses in More's poem, the illuminator has included the Tudor rose and the crown, the fleur-de-lis and the portcullis, as well as Catherine's pomegranate, in his design.
The British Library, Cotton MS Titus D.iv, f. 12v

ex libris survive (such an inscription would have been unusual in the period), there are other ways of identifying books she owned or read or which were associated with her queenship. First and foremost are those dedicated to her or to her and Henry conjointly or which carry an interlinked HK in their decoration. (97) For example, the text of Sir Thomas More's Coronation Day verses is accompanied by ornamentation featuring emblems of both Henry and Catherine. (98) In the prefatory letter More ironically blames the tardiness of the offering on the gout suffered by the illuminator. The flattery of Henry is to some degree undercut by the classical allusions and can possibly be read in an ambiguous light, but the poems are straightforward in their sympathy to Catherine, More's imagery suggesting a sadness in her life up to now, the men surrounding her less than trustworthy. In some sense, then, this volume prefigures the close bond which would develop between Catherine and More, a bond which would mature into a strong working relationship during the course of which the queen would on more than one occasion request the services of his pen.

Also in 1509 Piers de Champaigne, esquire of the body to Henry VIII, commissioned a book by the first King's Printer, William Faques, which contained a nicely matched set of texts, one concerning the care of the body, *De salute corporis*, by Willelmus de Saliceto, and one concerning the salvation of the soul, *De salute anime*, by Johannes de Turrecremata. The book was dedicated conjointly to Henry and Catherine; the presentation copy

99. This is the first printed book to celebrate the royal marriage: Henry's arms are found on the title page, Catherine's on the verso. Note also the inventory number, no. 864, identifying it as a Westminster book.
The British Library,
C.37.f.8, title page and verso

was printed on very high-quality paper, the fore-edge gilded. (99) As with the More poems, it stands as an exemplum of the public joy felt at the marriage: the union was seen as marking a new age of peace and prosperity.

In the library at Hatfield House there is an elegant manuscript of the Acts and Apocalypse, written by Pieter Meghen and decorated by a member of the Horenbout family, who were Flemish miniaturists. This manuscript forms part of a set, but unlike the others, which were prepared for John Colet, this one was intended for Henry and Catherine, whose initials, linked by true-love knots on a ground of green and white, the Tudor colours, are found in the border design. (101) Meghen, who wished to become 'Writer of the King's Books', included Catherine in the design because she was known to be sympathetic to this sort of material – the translation is by Jerome and Erasmus – as well as being a mediator for literary patronage with the king.

The arms of Sir John Donne, an administrator in Calais under Edward IV, Richard III and Henry VII, are found in three Flemish manuscripts. The grandest of these is a copy of Quintus Curtius Rufus's *Res gestae Alexandri Magni* ('The Deeds of Alexander the Great') in the French translation undertaken by Vasco de Lucena for Charles of Burgundy and presented in 1468, the year of his marriage to Margaret of York, sister of Edward IV. Donne's copy came to him from Guillaume de la Baume, who probably gave it in 1477 during the time when both men were involved in

100. Margaret of York describes herself to Donne in English as 'on of yor treu frendes' and Mary of Burgundy in French as 'vostre bonne amie'.
The British Library,
Royal MS 15.D. IV, f. 219

marriage negotiations on behalf of Mary of Burgundy, Margaret's stepdaughter. Margaret and Mary have inscribed affectionate messages to Donne in the manuscript. (100) On the same folio as the inscriptions has been added a coloured panel, related in style to those found in More's coronation manuscript, filled with Catherine and Henry's emblems, rose and pomegranate. No doubt the manuscript was presented to the royal couple by one of Donne's sons, perhaps the younger, Griffith, who was a skilled jouster, participating in the coronation tournament and the Westminster tournament of 1511 which celebrated the birth of the short-lived Prince Henry.

101. Here St Luke is shown
writing the Acts of the Apostles,
his emblem, the ox, beside him.
By courtesy of The Marquess of Salisbury,
Cecil Papers MS 324, f. 4

Catherine herself commissioned books or had books presented to her.
The English anti-Lutheran campaign began in good earnest on 12 May
1521, when Thomas Wolsey presided over a book burning in St Paul's
courtyard. By the king's own account it was Wolsey who encouraged the
composition of the *Assertio septem sacramentorum aduersus Martinum Lutherum*,
which appeared later that summer and which won Henry his coveted title of
Defender of the Faith. Predictably, Luther responded to the attack and
rather sharply, too, declaring that the *Assertio* proved the old adage that there
are no greater fools than kings and princes; that Henry was an ass, a pig, a
drunkard, a dreamer, mad and a most ignorant monster. After this lambast-
ing Henry quite wisely withdrew from the unseemly fray, leaving More and
John Fisher to take up the cause, More's *Response* to Luther and Fisher's
Confutation both appearing in 1523. In 1525 Fisher wrote a *Defensio regiae*

assertionis, of which Henry's copy still survives; it was conceived both as an attack on Luther's eucharistic doctrine and a defence of the king's *Assertio*. In the 1520s, then, Lady Margaret's old chaplain and spiritual advisor commanded the respect and enjoyed the intimacy of both her grandson and her granddaughter-in-law equally. His fall, less than a decade later, would have been difficult to predict at this point.

Although Henry's *Assertio* concerned itself primarily with the seven sacraments there was also a section defending indulgences against Luther's attack on this highly lucrative practice. Picking up on this aspect of the dispute, Catherine's Spanish confessor, Alphonsus de Villa Sancta, published, also in 1523, his *Problema indulgentiarum aduersus Lutherum*, which was dedicated to the queen as Defendress of the Faith. As this epithet – echoing Henry's own title – indicates, Villa Sancta, like Erasmus before him, saw Henry and Catherine as a matched intellectual/theological team. The *Problema indulgentiarum* appears twice in the Westminster inventory of 1542, and no doubt separate presentation copies were prepared for king and queen. One copy was missing by the time of Henry's death – beside the entry a later hand has written 'Deficit this booke' – and the other later migrated to Lambeth Palace. This second copy is still in the original cover: a panel binding owned by John Reynes with the royal arms on one side – the supporters being the dragon and greyhound, not the later dragon and lion – and a Tudor rose with surrounding motto on the other, Catherine's pomegranate at the bottom. Later in 1523 another polemical text by Villa Sancta dedicated to Catherine was published: entitled the *De libero arbitrio aduersus Melanchthonem*, it was his defence of free will against the Lutheran doctrines of grace adopted by Philipp Melanchthon. This tract seems to have signalled the serious commencement of the literary campaign against Luther, and Henry as well as Catherine may have been involved in its production. As with the *Problema* there were two copies at Westminster in 1542 and one has subsequently been lost. The other still survives in the British Library and, unusually for British Library books, it has not been rebound: it is in a panel binding which combines in one panel the two covers of the previous book. (102)

In his prefaces Villa Sancta observed that Catherine was much concerned with the 'Luther' problem and discussed the topic with him often. These two books provide material proof of her involvement in Henry's campaign to maintain orthodoxy and they are also fine witnesses to the

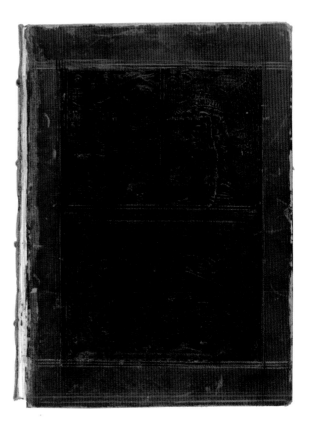

102. This panel was not cut until about 1522. After Catherine's fall the pomegranate was removed from the panel and replaced by the cock, one of Henry's badges.
The British Library, C.47.g.2, cover

accuracy of Erasmus's statement that Catherine was equal with the king in his struggle against heresy. If not intentional, then it is at least emblematic that eleven of the known copies of Henry's *Assertio* are bound with precisely the same binding as would be used for the *Problema indulgentiarum*: the works make a nicely balanced pair at all sorts of levels.

As is well known, Catherine was hugely concerned about education, in particular the education of women, and in 1523 – her *annus mirabilis* in terms of literary production – she invited her fellow countryman, Juan Luis Vives, to come to England from the Netherlands. Vives, who would act as tutor to Princess Mary in 1527 and 1528, wrote two tracts on female eduction at Catherine's behest: first, specifically for the edification of Princess Mary, *De ratione studii puerilis* ('On the Right Method of Instruction for Children'), published in 1524; secondly, and more generally directed, *De institutione foeminae Christianae* ('The Instruction of a Christian Woman'), presented in April 1523 and printed in 1524. In this latter work Vives praised Catherine's own upbringing; he also explained that he had been inspired 'by the favour, love and zeal that your Grace beareth to holy study and learning'; and he observed that the queen would see her own 'visage and image' reflected in the tract.

The *De institutione* contains some revolutionary statements about women's education in terms of accepted practice in northern Europe: Vives believed, for example, that girls should be taught grammar and rhetoric, scripture and moral philosophy. Education, in his opinion, was the best tool with which to combat the natural tendency in children of both sexes towards evil. He recommended a list of Latin texts for his royal charge – these included the Bible, the church fathers, and the moral philosophers of the ancient world – and his proposed reading list corresponds fairly closely to the books with which the library in Mary's favoured residence, New Hall in Essex, would later be stocked. On the other hand, he warned – as would Elizabeth's tutor Roger Ascham in the next generation – that vernacular romances should be eschewed as morally suspect. Catherine was mightily pleased with the book and she gave a copy to Sir Thomas More, himself much involved in the education of his daughters, asking him to provide a translation into English. More in turn passed this request on to Richard Hyrde, a tutor in his household and friend of John Leland, and Hyrde produced a version entitled *A very frutefull and pleasant boke called the Instruction of A Christian Woman*. In his preface Hyrde emphasized that nothing 'is more fruitful than the good education and order of women, the one half of all mankind, and that half also whose good behaviour or evil tatches affect for better or for worse the other half'. Both original and translation were at Westminster in 1542 and the presentation copy of the Latin text is now found in the Bodleian. The title page has been attractively hand-coloured and it is an altogether pleasing book to examine, deeply moving as a tangible reminder of Catherine's hopes and aspirations, just at the last moment before they would be shattered. (103)

Like both her husband and daughter, Catherine was drawn to music, and her maître de salle, Francisco Filippo, sent her back a group of eight Spanish minstrels on one of his missions to Spain. Catherine herself can be associated with music books, including a unique version of a complete cycle of Lady Mass settings by Nicholas Ludford, a Westminster musician employed by the Royal Free Chapel of St Stephen. The binding of each of the four volumes of the set consists of a panel incorporating devices of Henry and Catherine. The music was almost certainly used in one of the royal chapels, possibly in conjunction with Catherine's private devotions. After her fall the books were removed to Westminster, an inventory number inserted, and they appear in the 1542 inventory as 'Bookes of pricksong masses foure'.

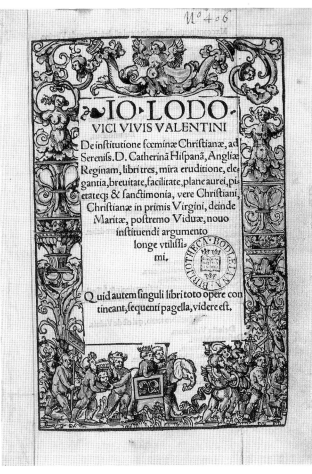

Another music book produced during Catherine's reign, now The British Library, Royal MS 11 E.XI, contains a double canon, *Salue radix*, with two notated voices, each of which is written around a finely painted Tudor rose. On the elaborate opening page appears a castle, the flags of England and Spain flying from two matching towers. Catherine is thus signalled in the design as Princess of Castile, of which her mother had been queen in her own right. By one interpretation, the volume was put together in 1513 when Henry was in the Low Countries campaigning against the French, and Catherine was acting as regent at home. In August came the victory of the Battle of the Spurs and the surrender of Thérouanne; in September Tournai fell, and Henry made a victorious

103. This copy of *De institutione* was acquired by the antiquary Richard Rawlinson, who realized that it was probably the presentation copy. The identifying Westminster inventory number, no. 406, is clearly visible.
Bodleian Library, Oxford, Bodl. Arch B.e.30, title page

entry on 25 September. These events, complemented by the defeat of the Scottish army and the death of James IV at Flodden Field, led to a number of artistic productions of which this could have been a prime example. Several of the poems are in praise of the Virgin Mary and it has also been suggested the volume in its present form represents an oblique tribute to Mary's birth on 8 February 1516 (and 1516 is inscribed on the front flyleaf). Theodor Dumitrescu has noted, however, that Henry and his sisters were reunited for the first time in nearly thirteen years in 1516, soon after Mary's birth, and that there were grand celebrations to commemorate the reunion, both in May and at Epiphany [1516 old style]. The iconography both of text and of design seems to make oblique reference to these celebrations; the tree on the opening page being especially appropriate with its marguerite (for Margaret), and marigold (for Mary), as well as Henry's crowned Tudor

104. The walled garden surrounded by waters represents England, which is saluted by the text on the castellated gateway, whose portcullis symbolizes the Beaufort line.
The British Library,
Royal MS 11.E.XI, f. 2r

105. Catherine's pomegranate has been combined in a rather provocative manner with Henry's Tudor rose.
The British Library, Royal MS 8.G.VII, ff. 2v–3r

rose. (104) No doubt, then, this manuscript stands as a tribute to a year of general rejoicing for king and queen and the Tudor dynasty in general.

Petrus Alamire, music copyist and spy, was responsible for a group of books illuminated in the Ghent–Bruges style so popular with the early Tudors. Probably composed at some point between 1510 and 1520, one of these contains twenty-eight motets, six Latin secular works and one canon (inserted into the manuscript in the seventeenth century). The first gathering has been designed to honour Henry and Catherine, as is apparent from their emblems and the royal coat of arms. (105) In the text itself there are five settings in a row of *Dulces exuuiae*, Dido's last lament from Book IV of Virgil's *Aeneid*. The musicologist Richard Sherr has recently argued in an unpublished paper that by the late 1520s the obvious analogies between Catherine and Dido – both widows abandoned by men who did not recognize the validity of the unions into which they had entered – could have turned this manuscript from a source of delight into an instrument of oppression, 'part of the psychological warfare that was being practiced on the poor queen'. Whether or not this interpretation actually applies to this particular manuscript, the analogues between Catherine and Dido are certainly striking ones.

In 1524 Catherine commissioned Erasmus to write a book on Christian marriage for her daughter, as a guide for her future career. The presentation copy of the resulting treatise, *Christiani matrimonii institutio* ('Institution of Christian Marriage') still survives in Emmanuel College Cambridge; by the time the text was published in 1526, however, it cannot have appealed either to the queen, since it had a section on annulment, or her husband, who was visibly chafing under the yoke of matrimony. (106) Erasmus, ever a pragmatist, did not show himself a particularly loyal friend to Catherine in the following years and when scholars were put in a position where they had to declare for Henry or for Catherine, Erasmus acted in a remarkably uncommittal, even cynical manner, suggesting in a letter sent to Vives in September 1528 that it would be better for Jove to take two Junos than to put one away. In the same month he wrote to William Blount, Lord Mountjoy, Catherine's chamberlain, recommending that Catherine read his *Vidua Christiana* ('On Christian Widowhood'), hardly a tactful suggestion in the context of Catherine's defence of her status as Henry's wife rather than Arthur's widow. Nevertheless, Catherine continued to respect and support Erasmus even in her darkest days, sending him gifts of money in 1528 and 1529. On her deathbed she was fortified by his *De preparatione ad mortem* ('On Preparation for Death'), ironically a work commissioned by Thomas Boleyn, the father of her bitter rival, to whom Erasmus referred in another book published in the same year as 'the most gracious and virtuous Queen Anne'.

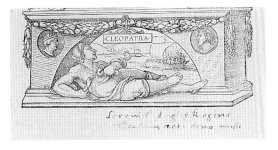

106. Erasmus has personally dedicated the book to Catherine: 'Serenissimae Anglie Reginae Erasmus Roterdami dono misit'. Reproduced by permission of the Master and Fellows of Emmanuel College, Cambridge, MSS 3.2.30, title page

Unlike Erasmus, Mountjoy remained consistent in his loyalty to his former patron. In 1533 he led an abortive mission, no doubt repugnant to him, to the remote hunting lodge at Ampthill in Bedfordshire where Catherine had recently been sent, asking Catherine to submit to the inevitable and acknowledge herself Dowager Princess. After this unsavoury and unsuccessful episode he wrote to Thomas Cromwell requesting to be replaced as chamberlain, pointing out his conflict of interest and observing that 'hit is not my parte, nor for me this often to vexe or unquyet her whom the kynges grace cawsed to be sworne unto and truly to serve her to my power'.

On 8 January 1536, Catherine died a lonely death in the place of her final banishment at Kimbolton Castle near Peterborough, surrounded by neither friends nor the trappings of royalty. Until she was repudiated, her official residence in London had been Baynard's Castle, which passed from her to Anne Boleyn, and then would go to Henry's subsequent wives. On 14 February 1536, just over a month after Catherine's death, Sir Edward Baynton, her former vice chancellor, who now occupied the same position in Anne's household, took an inventory of those of her possessions which remained at Baynard's Castle: these were to go to Henry (although many items were in fact 'delyvered to the Queane' – i.e. Anne). Amongst Catherine's goods were books: 'a primer, written in vellom, covered withe clothe of golde, having two claspis of silver and gilte'; 'three bookes covered withe red lether, garnysshid withe golde foyle, and tyed with grene reabande'; and 'seevyntene other bookys, smalle and greate, lockid in a cheste'. Like many of her other chattels, these books probably ended up at Westminster and the vellum primer, or Book of Hours, with a clothofgold binding is perhaps the lost no. 671 in the inventory – 'Primer written, coverid with cloth of golde' (108) – it was no doubt destroyed at the time of the Edwardian injunction of 25 February 1551 'for the purging of his Highnes Librarie at Westminster of all superstitiouse bookes, as masse bookes, legendes, and suche like'. The three books in red leather may well have been devotional books, remarkable primarily for the designs on their bindings, but it is impossible to ascertain their identity. The seventeen books in the chest, on the other hand, lead us to other titles in the 1542 inventory, books which confirm and deepen the conventional view of Catherine's abilities and interests, that is, a woman musically sophisticated and pious; 'of great sense and saintliness', as Erasmus would say in a letter to Petrus Mosellanus in 1519, 'and not unlearned'; a good wife and mother, whose mind turned seriously to book patronage in the early 1520s, when she was in her late thirties, unlikely to conceive again, and concerned with two related issues – heresy and the possibility of a female succession in England.

Amongst Latin authors Sallust was much admired by humanists and Lorenzo Valla provided a learned commentary to his writings in the fifteenth century. In the 1542 inventory there is a copy of his works, now lost, which almost certainly belonged to Catherine, since the volume, a sammelband (the technical term for disparate books bound together), also contained 'songis in spanysh'. The Sallust itself may have been the popular Spanish translation of Francisco Vidal de Noya, archdeacon of Burgos, first printed in 1493 and reissued several times, although it could equally well have been in Latin. Catherine also owned works by two of the most influential poets of the European Middle Ages: Dante and Petrarch. In 1515 Pedro

Fernando de Villegas's glossed verse translation into Castilian of the *Inferno*, dedicated to Juana de Aragon, duchesse de Frias, was printed in Burgos. Catherine's copy, described in the Westminster inventory as 'Dantis workes in the Castilian tonge' still survives in the British Library, although there are no notes in her hand and the inventory number, no. 222, has been trimmed in the process of rebinding. No doubt it was dispatched to Catherine fairly soon after its publication and it shows that she was assiduous in keeping up her Spanish connections after her settlement in England.

Like Dante's, Petrarch's writings enjoyed a considerable vogue in the early modern period: the *Trionfi* was one of his most popular works, and it was translated into a number of languages, including an English version for the king by Lord Morley. Catherine possessed a copy in the 1512 Castilian translation of Antonio de Obregón as *Los seys triunfos*: it contains a Westminster inventory number and an HR monogram associated with thirty-six Henrician books, the majority of which were in the vernacular. (107)

Printing dates suggest that these two books came to Catherine in her heyday, when fortune smiled. In her time of troubles she turned, humanistically trained as she had been, even more fervently to books, acquiring the Spanish translation of Erasmus's *Enchiridion militis Christiani* ('Manual for a Christian Soldier'), published in 1527, the year in which Henry began seriously to consider the annulment of their marriage. Another book from which Catherine drew solace was Petrarch's *De remediis utriusque fortunae* (*Remedies for Fortune Fair and Foul*, as it was called in an early translation), which she possessed in the Castilian translation of Francisco de Madrid – like *Los seys triunfos* it has the HR monogram on the title page. Her copy was published in Saragossa in 1518; she presumably obtained it soon after publication, but the text – like Dido's lament – took on new resonance when things started to go drastically wrong for her, and in 1527 (her *annus horribilis*) she requested Sir Thomas Wyatt to make an English translation. In the event, Wyatt did not complete the task: he claimed that the chore became tedious in its execution, but he may also have become uncomfortable with the text in the unfolding political situation. Instead, he presented Catherine on New Year's Day 1528 with Plutarch's *De tranquillitate et securitate animi* translated into English as *The Quyete of Mynde* – a work which preached the quietism and passive acceptance which was generally being recommended, completely unsuccessfully, to the formidable queen.

FRANCISCO DE LABARCA con los seys triunfos de toscano sacados en castellano con el comento que sobrellos se hizo. Con preuilegio Real.

107. The precise function of this HR monogram – standing for Henricus Rex – remains unknown and there is no clearly discernible pattern in the small group of books in which it occurs.
The British Library, C.63.i.10, title page

In the spring of 1531 the *Grauissimae atque exactissimae illustrissimarum totius Italiae et Galliae academiarum censurae* was published, ostensibly proving that the majority of the international academic community judged Henry's marriage to be invalid. By this date Henry's advisors were becoming increasingly aware of the potential of the printing press as a tool of propaganda and it was judged prudent to have the text made available in the vernacular for a general readership, especially since many Englishmen were showing themselves tenaciously loyal to Catherine. Not surprisingly, therefore, the Latin edition was followed in the next year by an English translation by Thomas Cranmer. In spite of Cranmer's efforts, as we have seen, books in favour of Catherine continued to appear. One of these, specifically described in its

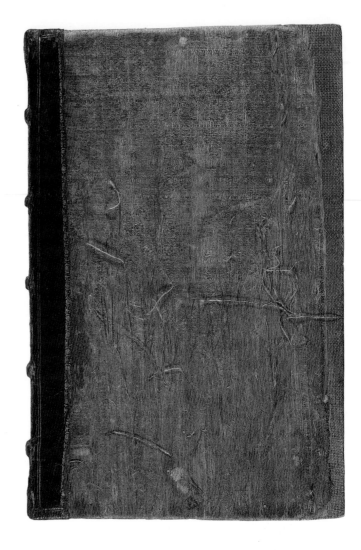

108. The is one of the rare
surviving Henrician books to
retain its cloth‑of‑gold covering.
The President and Fellows of
Magdalen College, Cambridge,
Pepys MS 1760, cover

title as a confutation of the determinations and a defence of the pope's right
to dispense in cases of a dead brother's widow – i.e. *Non esse neque diuino
neque naturae iure prohibitum quin Summus Pontifex dispensare possit ut frater demor‑
tui sine liberis fratris uxorem legitimo matrimonio sibi possit adiungere, aduersus aliquot
academiarum censuras tumultuaria ac perbreuis apologia siue confutatio* – was pub‑
lished anonymously, perhaps in Antwerp, in 1532. Reminding Henry of his
role as Defender of the Faith, the author blamed the present 'tragedy' on bad
counsellors and he demonstrated how seemingly contradictory Old Testa‑
ment texts could be reconciled to uphold the validity of the king's marriage
to Arthur's widow. *Non esse* has been attributed to Catherine's old client
Juan Luis Vives – who had lost Henry's favour by supporting Catherine's
position on the divorce question and had then alienated Catherine herself
by advocating a policy of non‑aggression – but it is not likely that he was the
author. One of the few surviving copies is now at Lambeth Palace, to
which it was removed with many other royal books in the early seventeenth

century by Richard Bancroft, archbishop of Canterbury. The Lambeth copy has many marginalia: although each flattering comment about the king's orthodoxy has been noted with approval, the annotator stands firmly behind Catherine and 'Pro coniuga regis Katherina' ('For Catherine, *wife* to the king') has been written on the title page.

After her death Catherine came to be associated with the passive suffering Wyatt obliquely advocated and she was identified on more than one occasion with a literary figure well known to Chaucerians: patient Griselda who tolerated without complaint, but also without bending, any cruelty her husband might inflict upon her. In 1539 Vives compiled a Latin grammar for older schoolboys, *Linguae Latinae exercitatio* ('The Practice of the Latin Language'), in which a model house was described. In the dining room hang three pictures: (i) Griselda; (ii) St Godelieve of Flanders, strangled by her tyrannical husband; and (iii) Catherine of Aragon. Henry still alive, Vives dared not press the analogy further, but during Mary's reign William Forrest could afford to be more specific and he wrote a complete treatise on the topic, *A True and Most Notable History of the Right, Noble and Famous Lady, produced in Spain, entitled the Second Gresyld*. Reality, of course, was crueller than the fairy tale, in which the tyrannical Walter was transformed to a dutiful husband, deeply admiring of his stoical and highly principled wife.

As early as 1530, the Italian Carmelite Giacomo Calco recommended that Henry adopt an Old Testament type when confronting the papacy and cast himself as Susannah on account of her resistance to the Elders – better to be excommunicated (or worse), in other words, than to disobey the dictates of one's conscience. The mind boggles at the thought of Henry as a modern Susannah who, in fact, provides a better analogy for Catherine, one of whose last public acts shows very strong parallels with this biblical prototype. In many ways Catherine saw her grandmother-in-law, Lady Margaret Beaufort, as a kind of role model. Deeply pious, Lady Margaret had been assiduous in the distribution of royal alms on Maundy Thursday. As queen, Catherine also kept her Maundy – a royal prerogative and thus symbolically important – but Henry did not wish her to continue the practice as Princess Dowager. In the last year of her life Henry ordered Sir Edmund Bedingfield, steward of her household, to stop her. When prohibited, Catherine responded that 'in her conscyence she was bound to kepe a maundy in the honor of God, making hole provysyon for the same at her owen charge, and further sayeng that my Lady the Kinges graunt dame duryng her lyfe kept a yerly maundy'. In panic Bedingfield and a colleague contacted the king's secretary, Stephen Gardiner, desiring 'that we maye be advertesyd of the Kinges pleasure on this behalf with all dilygence'. It is not clear what happened next, but it seems likely that this is one of the many occasions on which Henry had to submit to the queen's stronger and less flexible conscience in spite of all his loud blusterings.

As Catherine of Aragon's star was falling, so too was Anne Boleyn's rising and the writings of Sir Thomas Wyatt provide a neat link between the two women. For the former Wyatt recommended stoic tranquillity of mind, for the latter he possibly translated love sonnets from Petrarch, full of coded language and double entendres. Nowadays most people see Anne through Wyatt's eyes and as represented by the court painters – the beautiful face, swanlike neck, and a golden B, if not a scarlet A, upon her chest – inevitably contrasting her with the matronly Spanish queen. (110, 111) Anne, it is clear, loved jewels and beautiful objects, including elaborate bindings. In May 1531 the king's Flemish goldsmith, Cornelius Hayes, submitted a bill for the past year, consisting primarily of items for Anne, which included: 'mending a little book which was garnished in France', and 'garnishing a little book with crown gold for her'. In 1534 Hayes was commissioned to provide an elaborate cradle for the anticipated boy child; he also presented a bill for 'the garnishing of two books with silver gilt, 66 oz, at 6s. For the books and binding 41s. To Mr Loke [i.e. Sir William Locke, gentleman usher of the chamber] for the velvet that covered the books, 43s. 9d.' There is evidence to suggest that these same books were sequestered after Anne's downfall: among the goods brought to the Jewel House in the Tower from Windsor after Henry's own death were 'foure bookes whereof three are covered with vellat and one with tynsell. One of them is garnished with A crowned and one other of gold H and A. The third of silver and gilte and H and A and the fourthe with white silver.' Of the nine or so surviving books which can be associated with Anne, moreover, those which retain their original bindings closely match these descriptions in one way or another.

The actual contents of Anne's books, however, give a differing impression of Anne's character from that conveyed by the bindings, one which matches more closely the descriptions by her supporters – her chaplain, William Latymer, reporting that she was 'very experte in the Frenche tounge, exercising her selfe contynually in reading the Frenche Bible and other Frenche bookes of *like effecte*' (my emphasis), and the Protestant martyrologist John Foxe later describing her as a pious woman who 'delighted in doing good' and who was greatly loved by the nation.

Anne spent her formative years at the French court, where she became acquainted with Francis I's sister, the deeply pious Marguerite de Navarre. Long after her return to England Anne continued to foster this connection: in 1532, for example, she fervently hoped that Marguerite would come to Calais to meet her and Henry; such a meeting, she believed, would give a kind of *imprimatur* to the forthcoming marriage. In 1535 Anne sent a message to Marguerite paying her the highest tribute possible by stating that her 'greatest wish, next to having a son, was to see you again'. Politically astute, Marguerite was a learned woman who surrounded herself with intellectuals

of a reformist character. One of these was the evangelical scholar, Jacques
Lefèvre d'Etaples (c.1460–1536), whose translations of the Bible into
French were printed in Antwerp by Martin Lempereur, the man also
responsible for the production of William Tyndale's New Testament in
English. Anne and Henry conjointly owned a copy of one of these translations bound in two volumes. (114) Another of Anne's
books is a manuscript copy of an evangelical tract in
French, perhaps by Marguerite's protégé, Clément Marot,
concerning 'Le Pasteur évangélique' ('The Evangelical
Pastor'), presented to her between 1533 and 1536. (109) In
his introduction the author flatteringly pairs Henry and
Francis, Anne and Marguerite. The manuscript contains an
illustration of Anne's badge of a crowned falcon, which,
according to one interpretation, is also found, viciously
pecking a pomegranate, in the famous music book associated with her, now Royal College of Music, MS 1070. In
fact this manuscript, consisting of thirty-nine Latin motets
and five French chansons, was probably produced in
France in the second decade of the sixteenth century, and
came into Anne's possession well before she became the
object of Henry's desires.

ANNE BOLEYN

Yet another of Anne's books is a French psalter copied
at Rouen and illuminated by an individual known as the
Ango Master between December 1529 and September
1532, before Anne became queen but while Henry was
actively courting her. Part of the design includes a cipher which turns up
elsewhere and whose reading is almost certainly HENricus REX, Sovereign Lord. The translation itself is perhaps by Louis de Berquin, who was
executed in Paris in 1529 for his pro-Lutheran views. Berquin's writings
were published by the well-known printer of evangelical texts, Simon Du
Bois, who moved from Paris to Alençon around 1529; sheltering under the
direct patronage of Marguerite herself he soon came to the attention of
Anne and her brother George, Viscount Rochford.

109. The arms assigned to
Anne Boleyn as queen are
prominently displayed, in
'Le Pasteur évangélique'.
Later at Westminster, the
manuscript was no. 463
in the 1542 inventory.
The British Library,
Royal MS 16.E.XIII, f. IV

Heraldic devices are especially prominent in the two most visually exciting and elaborately decorated of Anne's books – a matched pair, copied by
the same scribe and produced by Flemish-trained craftsmen working in
England. Now in the Harley Collection in the British Library, the earlier
and less ornate of the two was prepared for Anne during the brief period
after she was created Marquess of Pembroke on 1 September 1532, but before
she was recognized as queen in March 1533. (112) Marking the preface is a
coroneted lozenge with Anne's arms situated in a square frame divided ver-
tically argent, or, sable with a canton sinister. In the lower corners of the
frame and to the left and right beneath the coronet the HENREXSL cipher
occurs. (113) The actual text derives from a printed book, the *Epistres et
evangiles des cinquante et deux sepmaines de l'an* ('Epistles and Gospels for the
Fifty-two Weeks of the Year'), assembled by Lefèvre d'Etaples and his disci-
ples. It consists of the Epistle and Gospel readings for the year, each followed

110. This is an example of the standard image of Anne Boleyn, one which exemplifies Wyatt's literary portrait. It is probably an authentic likeness.

Dean and Chapter of Ripon

111. Attributed to Lucas Horenbout, this portrait of Catherine dates to 1525–27, at precisely the point when Henry was deciding that his first marriage might well be invalid.

National Portrait Gallery, 4682

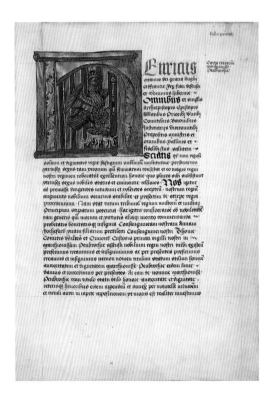

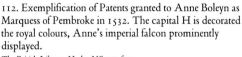

112. Exemplification of Patents granted to Anne Boleyn as Marquess of Pembroke in 1532. The capital H is decorated the royal colours, Anne's imperial falcon prominently displayed.

The British Library, Harley MS 303, f. 1r

113. Anne Boleyn's arms: Brotherton, gules, 3 lions passant guardant or, a label argent; Warenne chequy or and argent (arms of the Earls of Surrey); Ormonde, or, a chief indented azure; Rochford argent, a lion rampant sable, crowned gules.

The British Library, Harley MS 6561, f. 2r

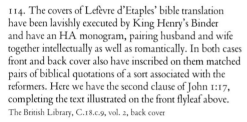

114. The covers of Lefèvre d'Etaples' bible translation have been lavishly executed by King Henry's Binder and have an HA monogram, pairing husband and wife together intellectually as well as romantically. In both cases front and back cover also have inscribed on them matched pairs of biblical quotations of a sort associated with the reformers. Here we have the second clause of John 1:17, completing the text illustrated on the front flyleaf above.

The British Library, C.18.c.9, vol. 2, back cover

115. The binding of *The Ecclesiaste* is rich in symbolism: the bosses illustrate the crowned lion rampant guardant, the dragon, the crowned falcon on roses and the greyhound; there are decorated brass clasps, and in the centre a shield in enamel, Henry's arms impaling Anne's, surmounted by a crown.

Collection of the Duke of Northumberland, Percy MS 465, cover

by a short homily; the latter translated into English in the Harley manuscript. Based on the principle that the Gospel should be accessible to the laity and emphasizing the centrality of Christ above the traditions of the church, the *Epistres et evangiles* was condemned by the Sorbonne, alert to its possible Lutheran echoes, but nevertheless it survives in at least seven editions up to 1551, two published by Du Bois. The actual printed book from which this particular manuscript was copied also survives; in 1536 it was sequestered into the royal library along with the other books belonging to the Boleyn siblings.

Written while Anne was queen, *The Ecclesiaste* is now at Alnwick Castle. Probably acquired by the son of the sixth duke of Northumberland, who succeeded to the title in 1899, it was of interest to the family because of the early romantic association of Anne Boleyn with Henry, the sixth earl of Northumberland. Precisely when it left the royal library is unknown. Even grander than the Harley manuscript, *The Ecclesiaste* retains its original bind-ing (black velvet, now faded to grey-brown, on wooden boards) with deco-ration containing royal badges. (115) In the manuscript itself there are a series of eight designs for major initials – some repeated several times – and these pay tribute to Anne: the first initial has Henry and Anne's arms; a second contains the HA monogram; a third shows her crowned falcon on red and white roses; (117) next comes a design featuring an anchor hanging from a celestial sphere. (118) The motto Anne adopted after her marriage, 'The Moste Happye' also appears, (120) as does a design featuring oak tree foliage; some initials have Anne's own shield crowned and there is a pattern with gold tracery.

As in the case of the Harley manuscript, the text of *The Ecclesiaste* is taken from a book printed by Simon Du Bois at Alençon. In the printed version the biblical text itself is presented in French, each verse followed by detailed exegesis (also in French) by the German evengelical Johannes Brenz, whose commentary emphasizes the pre-eminence of the Bible itself over the traditions and sacraments of the Church and ultimately derives from Luther's writings. The Alnwick manuscript leaves the text in French and translates the commentary into English.

Both these books are of a calibre normally commissioned only by royalty or the very highest levels of the aristocracy. In both cases the motifs employed in the decoration indicate intimacy with Anne. In each, the translator/donor has chosen a small and cheaply produced printed book – evangelical in tone and designed to make the scripture available to laymen (also easy to hide in the event of religious persecution) – for transformation into a deluxe manuscript. Who was he? Although his name does not appear in the badly water-damaged dedication page of the Harley manuscript – the preface to *The Ecclesiaste* is now missing – the author did refer to 'the perpetuall bond of blood' which linked him to his patron. In a passage which is only accessible by means of ultraviolet light, moreover, he declares himself to be Anne's 'moost lovyng and fryndely brother' and, in spite of doubts by some scholars, the reference must be a literal one, to Anne's brother George. There is also an identifying cipher. (121) That George Boleyn undertook this translation is not surprising. Fluent in French, he served in France on several diplomatic missions. Like Anne he was sympathetic to the strain of religious thought expressed in these two works and he formed part of her intimate coterie. Although George was well known and commended as a gentleman-scholar and poet even in his own lifetime, these two translations are, as it happens, the only writings which can indisputably be attributed to him. And in the speech he is reported to have made just before his execution he may have been making an oblique reference to them:

> … men do comon and saye that I have bene a settar forthe of the
> worde of God, and one that hath favored the Ghospell of Christ; and
> bycawse I would not that God's word shuld be slaundered by me, I
> say unto yow all, that yf I had followed God's worde in dede as I dyd
> rede it and set it forthe to my power, I had not come to this.

'Set it forthe' may well describe the translating activities he so actively (and learnedly) espoused.

In the early seventeenth century one Rose Hickman described how her father, Sir William Locke, supplier of velvet for bindings, brought foreign books to Anne: 'I remember that I have heard my father say that when he was a yong merchant and used to go beyond sea, Queene Anne Boloin that was mother to our late Queene Elizabeth caused him to get her the gospells and epistles written in parchment in French together with the psalms'. Both in iconography and in fact, imported books played a major role in Anne's court; they underline her cultural and religious orientation: France and evangelism. Nevertheless, the Du Bois imprints, of which she and her brother owned a number, were meant for 'les simples and les rudes' and were not appropriate for public show as part of the queen's symbolic representation of herself. (116) The production of deluxe manuscripts from these humble printed books indicates a conscious programme of transformation and elevation. Anne clearly was imitating the reformist atmosphere of Marguerite's court and visibly aligning herself with reform through the *reading and display* of these impressive manuscripts.

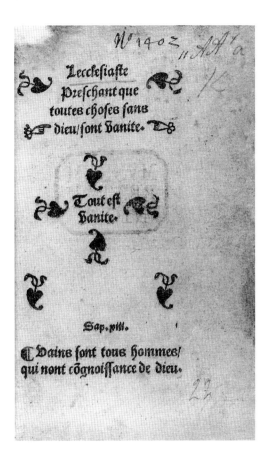

116. This modest printed book provided the text which was used as a basis for the grand Northumberland *Ecclesiaste* manuscript.
The British Library, 1016.a.5, title page

Why did George present his sister with bilingual texts when she could read French perfectly well, perhaps even better than English? To some extent, these may have been books whose role, apart from their iconographic function, would have been to provide pious material for Anne to read and discuss with her ladies, some of whom were no doubt monolingual. There may, however, be another motivation as well, one pertaining to the giver rather than the receiver. Translation, as we have seen, was an aristocratic accomplishment, and George's father-in-law, Lord Morley, translated texts from Latin to English for Mary, even though she knew Latin well. By its very nature a translation would be an entirely appropriate and rather smart gift from George to his sister. Moreover, although it introduces sober theological materials, the preface to the *Epistres et evangiles* reads like an exercise in the conventions of courtly love. It is full of compliments and elegantly expressed self-deprecation, beautifully set out in a well-balanced structure; a humble suppliant, George prays his sister 'paciently to pardon where any faute ys, allwayes consideryng that by your commandement I have adventuryd to do this, without the whiche it had not been in me to have perfourmyd yt. But that hath had pooire to make me passe my wit, which lyke as in this I have been redy to fulfyll, so in all other thynges at all tymes I shall be redy to obey.' If one did not know these were a brother's words, one could easily mistake them for those of a hopeful suitor. Coyly, too, George hints at Anne's upcoming marriage 'prayeng hym [Christ] oon whoome this booke treatyth to graunt you many good yeres to his plesure and shortely to encres in hartes easse with honnor [i.e. to become Henry's wife]'. This

117. This is a good rendition of Anne's device: a silver
falcon crowned gold, holding a gold sceptre in its right
talon, standing on a golden trunk out of which sprout
both red and white roses and the words 'Mihi et mea'.
The organ screen at King's College chapel employs this
motif and also has the HA monogram.
Collection of the Duke of Northumberland, Percy MS 465, f. 23r

119. Elsewhere one of Wyatt's witticisms appears to
be directed at the social upstart Smeaton: 'He that is an
ass, and thinks himself an hind, On leaping a ditch
will realize the truth'.
The British Library, Royal MS 20.B.XXI, rear flyleaf

118. The key to this design, as Anne Boleyn's biogra-
pher, Eric Ives, has pointed out, must lie in the interpretation of the '6H'. If the 6 really is a sigma, 'we have a
letter which was used in royal monograms to mean
"Sovereign". In that case, the religious level of meaning
is indicated by the monogram "IHS" for Jesus above the
central scroll, and the secular by "H" for "Henry,
Sovereign", below it, with the remaining symbols taking
on meanings appropriate to the respective levels'.
Collection of the Duke of Northumberland, Percy MS 465, f. 34r

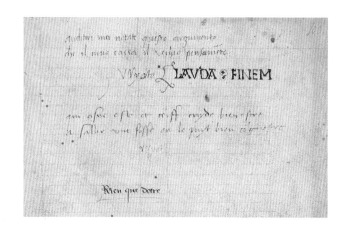

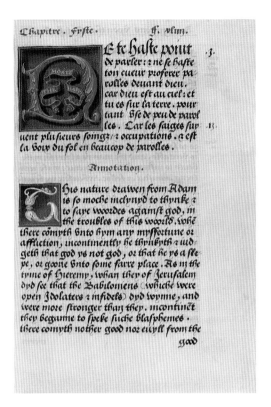

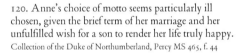

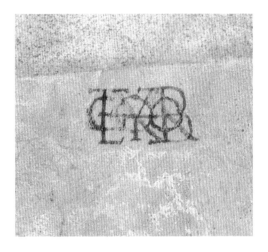

120. Anne's choice of motto seems particularly ill chosen, given the brief term of her marriage and her unfulfilled wish for a son to render her life truly happy.
Collection of the Duke of Northumberland, Percy MS 465, f. 44

121. The cipher on the first folio of the Harley manuscript contains letters for both Boleyn and George. Hans Holbein designed ciphers, several of which are almost identical to this in some of their letter forms and layout.
The British Library, Harley MS 6561, f. 1v

cryptic phrase must have struck a resonant chord when the newly created Marquess of Pembroke first read it.

In a sense, then, these two glorious manuscripts help reconcile the divided image of Anne which has troubled modern historians and biographers. On one hand, we do have elements of the 'frivolous butterfly' (as she has been described), whose household was a centre of elegant artifice, who owned and proudly flaunted her beautifully crafted, jewel-like books, 'gorgiously' bound, tributes from sophisticated admirers. Nevertheless, this is not incompatible with her self-representation as the pious follower of the teaching of the French reformers, an English version of Marguerite of Navarre. In both aspects the presence of her brother looms large.

Apart from translating fashionable reformist material for his sister, George may have gone further; he may even have persuaded her to show the truly revolutionary *Supplication for the Beggars* by the anticlerical lawyer Simon Fish – of which Anne apparently had a copy – to her theologically conservative husband. Nor was Fish the only evangelical writer for whom Anne served as a conduit to the king: William Marshall, Thomas Cromwell's client, dedicated his translation of the poor-relief regulations of Ypres to Anne, 'the flower of all queens', pleading with her 'to be a mediatrice and mean unto our most dread sovereign lord'. After having printed two leaves of his English translation of Genesis, the Cambridge reformer and translator George Joye, in exile at Bergen-op-Zoom, sent copies both to Henry and to the new queen in 1533. He also requested a licence to translate and print the whole Bible in English; but even under Anne's influence Henry was not yet ready for this step and so the project remained unachieved. At the very end of her reign, when her own position was precarious, Anne prudently refused to sponsor Thomas Revell's *The Sum of Christianity Gathered out almost of all Places of Scripture* (translated from the *Farrago Rerum Theologicarum* of the renegade Frenchman François Lambert and a categoric denial of the sacrifice of the Mass), in spite of the author's observation that in the past she had done much to 'promote, furder and sette forthe Goddes worde'. Open patronage of this kind of tract would indeed have confirmed the horrified condemnation by the imperial ambassador Eustace Chapuys of 'the heretical doctrines and practices of the concubine – the principal cause of the spread of Lutheranism in this country'.

The printed books from which George's gifts derive fit into a distinct group of almost twenty volumes in Henry's library, many in unique copies. The rarity of the Du Bois imprints in France is easy to explain – in the aftermath of the notorious rejection of the Real Presence by the organizers of the 'Affaire des Placards' this sort of material was uniformly destroyed – but why so many got to England has baffled book historians, who also question who might have been reading them. In fact, it must have been George or Anne who was having the books imported. Coming at the time of the break with Rome they stand in the most general sense as symbols of the emerging Church of England. The two surviving manuscripts also show George as more than a reader: he was an active adaptor, consciously identifying himself and his sister very firmly with a theological position, one which had strong links with the milieu of Marguerite.

The fact that this pair of manuscripts was abstracted from the royal library after the king's death may suggest that these were not the only ones to have been produced and there may have been others which have subsequently disappeared from the public domain (as the royal library ultimately became) or have been destroyed. There are certainly other indications that this sort of writing was circulating during Anne's ascendency. According to one of Thomas Cromwell's remembrances George Boleyn was required in 1534 to deliver a book in French to Francis I on Henry's behalf. What sort of *French* book would Henry be sending Francis through the agency of his brother-in-law? Quite possibly this was a manuscript, something similar in content and decoration to the ones that had come to Anne. If this is the case, it may well be that witnesses to printed books in French of an evangelical nature which, as we know from titles in Henry's booklists, once existed but which have disappeared without trace, may be found in manuscripts written posterior, rather than anterior to their printing, and deriving from the Boleyn circle, a circle in which brother and sister were equally active.

George Boleyn's wife managed to regain her position at court after his execution for alleged incest with his sister Anne and she had her living augmented to one hundred pounds per annum by her reluctant father-in-law, but she did not get back all her husband's goods, including his books. At least two of his manuscripts were at Westminster in 1542. Both in French, these add to our sense of George's cultural milieu, the world of Henry's minions, where chivalry and courtly romance formed the order of the day. The first is an older production, a fifteenth-century copy of the French translation of Matheolus of Bologna's satire on marriage and the response of the translator, Jean Le Fèvre, to the satire, which Boleyn owned by 1526. It was probably given to him in jest as a wedding gift, and, as it turns out, it was prophetic in a way he little imagined at the time, given his wife's testimony against him in 1536. Boleyn handed the book over to his young musician friend Mark Smeaton, later accused of being another of Anne's putative lovers, who wrote in it 'A moi M. Marc S'. The manuscript also has proverbs in Latin, French, and Spanish on the back flyleaves, along with the name 'Wyat'. (119) The second manuscript, now in the National Library of Scotland, is a copy of Ramón Lull's immensely popular *Libre del Orde de cavalleria* in an anonymous French translation, slightly reworked by the French physician, Symphorien Champier, as *Lordre de chevalrie*. Needless to say, this kind of text – a book of instruction on chivalry presented like a Rule by an older knight to a young squire – was precisely what would appeal to Henry's cronies and this copy was transcribed by Thomas Wall, Windsor herald, for Henry's brother-in-law Charles Brandon. Brandon then passed it on to Rochford, who proudly entered on the title page: 'This booke is myn George Rocheford'.

George and Anne Boleyn were an immensely attractive pair, intellectually and physically. Their world was a highly charged one, one in which the stakes were very high and alliances constantly shifting; it was the milieu bitterly rejected by Wyatt in 'Mine Own John Poins' just at the moment of its collapse: 'I cannot honor them that sets their part / With Venus and Bacchus all their life long / ... I cannot crouch nor kneel to do so great a wrong, / To worship them like God on earth alone, / That are as wolves these sely lambs among / ... The friendly foe, with his double face / Say he is gentle and courteous therewithal'. In this atmosphere drama and reality merge, historical fact and fiction become impossible to separate. After the fall of the Boleyns, the court became a much less glamorous place – or at least it did until Anne's daughter, 'Gloriana', found herself on the throne, surrounded by her own groups of competing and back-stabbing young men.

Because the royal household was constantly on the move, most books were stored in removing coffers rather than on shelves; the contents of these coffers were listed (usually not very helpfully, as we have seen) in the postmortem inventory, by which time they had been securely locked up in the Tower. The majority of the queen's books were described as 'litell' or 'very litell' and must have been girdle books. They were kept side by side with jewels, bottles, mirrors and other domestic items and were valued primarily for their elaborate bindings. This manifestation of the book as decorative object – something to be worn rather than read – provides the context for the list of five books given to Catherine Howard at the time of her marriage to Henry in 1540:

1 Item oone booke of golde ennamuled wherin is a clock. Upon every syde of which booke is thre diamondes, a litle man standing upon oone of them, foure turqueses and thre rubyes, with a litle cheyne of golde hanging at it ennamuled.
2 Item oone booke of golde ennamuled with blacke, garnesshed with xxvii rubyes, havyng also a cheyne of golde and perle to hange it by, conteignyng xliii peerlles.
3 Item oone other booke ennamuled with grene, white and blewe, havyng a feir sapher on euery syde and viii rubyes upon the same booke.
4 Item oone booke of golde ennamuled with blacke, white and red and garnesshed with viii small rubyes, havyng H.I. ennamuled with blacke, the backes of the same booke being glasse.
5 Item one booke of golde conteignyng xii diamondes and xl rubyes.

These bindings must have been extraordinarily ornate, studded with costly stones; indeed the first item was no doubt simply a case in a book-like shape. At least one of the books had been recycled – H I stands for Henry and Jane (Seymour). When Catherine fell into disgrace just over a year later, her possessions were sequestered and in the 1542 inventory of Westminster there is a reference to four other books which had once belonged to her:

1 Item oone masse booke coverid with purple vellat with claspes of copper.
2 Item oone other litle masse booke coverid with lether.
3 Item oone Newe Testament coverid with purple vellat gernysshid with silver and gilt with two claspes to the same of like silver and gilt.
4 Item oone litle Frenche booke coverid with crymsen vellat having two claspes of golde with these scripture 'Ihesus fiat uoluntas tua'.

Unlike those in the earlier list, these books were meant for consultation rather than wearing and would have been a more normal size – even the French book is little rather than very little in the manner of so many of the books in the queen's coffers. One of the books, the little Mass book, was bound in leather, a binding material which was coming more and more into vogue, and it would no doubt have had blind-stamped panels with heraldic designs. None of the books in these two lists has survived. Nor is this surprising: in Edward VI's reign there were specific injunctions instructing that any examples of this sort of papistical nonsense found in the royal library be destroyed, and Catherine's books doubtless fell victim to the fire in the same manner their owner fell to the headman's axe. Some of the bindings, on the other hand, would have been broken down, their jewels and precious metals recycled.

In 1604, Catherine's kinsman, Charles Howard, earl of Nottingham, the impecunious Lord High Admiral of England, was persuaded by Sir Thomas Bodley to hand over a group of fifty-two books, many of which still survive, to the latter's newly established library in Oxford. A number of these were previously owned by Henry, having been acquired by Nottingham's father William Howard, first baron Howard of Effingham, from the collection of one Sir Thomas Copley. Copley was a connection of the Boleyn family, who left England permanently in 1570 after openly espousing Roman Catholicism. He thus forfeited his lands and goods for life, William Howard directing the confiscations. Many years later, Copley's granddaughters, who were nuns at the Augustinian House of St Monica's in Louvain, referred specifically to the fate of their grandfather's library: 'so fair a library of books that [Howard] pleasured therewith the universities of England [i.e. the Bodleian]'. But how did Copley obtain them in the first place?

Fourteen of the books have been bound by King Henry's Binder and are stamped with the royal arms, the greyhound and dragon as supporters. All fourteen have had the initials KH embossed in them. KH cannot stand for 'King Henry' as some early scholars suggested – this is hopelessly anachronistic since the king's monogram was, as we have seen, invariably HR (i.e. Henricus Rex) – and K must represent Katherine. The fifteenth example with this same binding was at Westminster in 1542 and is a copy of a polemical treatise defending royal power against the church, *Opus eximium de uera differentia regiae potestatis et ecclesiasticae* ('An Excellent Work on the True Difference between Royal and Ecclesiastical Power'), by Edward Foxe, provost of King's College Cambridge and later bishop of Hereford. (122) Given that the *De uera differentia* was not printed until 1534, it obviously could not have been bound before then, and Catherine of Aragon can thus be eliminated as our ambiguous 'K', having been utterly and completely repudiated by Henry in the previous year. The *De uera differentia* can also be used to remove Henry's last queen as a candidate for ownership, since the book was already separated from the others and at Westminster in 1542 to be inventoried, that is before Catherine Parr was on the scene. By process of elimination, then, only Catherine Howard remains in the running and the Nottingham group must represent a set of books conjointly owned by the king and his fifth wife.

122. Printed on vellum, this
copy of the *De uera differentia*
carries the Westminster
inventory number, no. 253.
The British Library,
C.24.a. 25, cover

All in Latin, these books (with the exception of *De uera differentia*) con-
sist of works by the church fathers, most in Erasmus's up-to-date editions: a
two-volume set of Ambrose's *Omnia opera* (1527); a ten-volume set of
Augustine's *Omnia opera* (1528–29); a six-volume set of Jerome's *Omnia
Opera* (1524–26); a five-volume edition of the Greek father St John
Chrysostom (1523); and a single volume of works by Gregory the Great
(1523). Obviously, the books do not tie in with anything we know about
Catherine's tastes or inclinations, let alone linguistic abilities. Nor can one
imagine that the king was initiating a humanistic educational programme
for his new young bride. In fact, the only way to explain their existence is to
put them into the context of Henry's other shows of magnificence in the late
1530s and early 1540s, specifically, the ornately decorated palace at Nonsuch,
which Henry was completing at the time of his marriage to Catherine.
(123) No doubt these were books which Henry already had on hand – they

were just the sort of fashionable reading that would have been collected in the 1520s by a ruler priding himself on his learning – and he must have had them rebound in the heraldic manner which dominated at Nonsuch after he married Catherine. They were meant, then, to be displayed in the library, to be looked *at*, not *in*. Accordingly, they provide us with a very early example of buying, or at least binding, 'by the yard'. The books later came to Copley as a result of his well-documented friendship with the Keeper of the Palace at Nonsuch, Sir Thomas Cawarden, and were abandoned when he left the increasingly Protestant England of Elizabeth's reign.

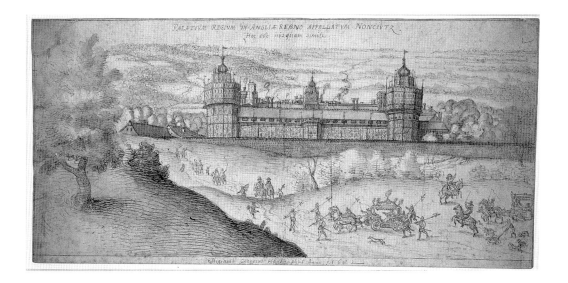

123. This view of Nonsuch from the south was executed by Joris Hoefnagel in 1568.
Department of Prints and Drawings, The British Museum

Although she inherited jewellery by the terms of Henry's will, Catherine Parr (d. 1548) never received the bulk of it. After the attainder and execution on 20 March 1549 of her fourth husband, Thomas Seymour, Lord High Admiral, the goods she did possess were removed from Sudeley Castle in a large chest or standard. On 16 November Sir John Thynne, Lord Protector Somerset's secretary, sent the keys to William Paulet, baron St John (later earl of Wiltshire and then marquess of Winchester), so an inventory could be made and then the coffer was transferred to the secret Jewel House in the Tower. One of the sixteen titles in the inventory – 'Newe Testament in Frenche covered with purple vellat garneshed with silver and gilte' – matches precisely the description of one of Catherine Howard's books, from whom no doubt it derived. Another had a superb binding: 'a booke of golde enameled blacke, garneshed with eighte and twentie small table rubies and one rocke rubie uppon the claspe and on eche side of the bok a table diamounte'. A third on vellum, perhaps even a manuscript, was written in Italian. Catherine prided herself on her Italian and in 1544 Princess Elizabeth wrote a letter to her in this language. One of Catherine's surviving printed books, a copy of Petrarch's *Canzoniere & Trionfi*, is also in Italian. (124) Apart from the Petrarch, a predictable and highly popular work in its original language or in translation (as is witnessed by the collections of both Catherine of Aragon and Henry), most of Catherine's books were devotional: books of prayers, psalms, a primer, copies of the New Testament in French and English, one inherited from her second husband, John Neville, third Lord Latimer. The biblical texts are especially significant in terms of her intellectual development, since in her *The Lamentation of a Sinner* (written in the winter of 1545–46 and published in 1547) she attributed her 'conversion' to reading the scriptures in translation, which she was in the habit of doing in the company of 'divers well learned and godly persons', whose chore it was to instruct her. Her copy of the 1542 translation of *A Sermon of Saint Chrysostome* by the Oxford scholar and friend of John Leland, Thomas Lupset, is now at Sudeley Castle: it has her signature 'Kateryn the Quene KP' on the title page.

Catherine, the only English queen whose writings have appeared in print in her own lifetime, ordered multiple copies of her own *Prayers or Medytacions, Wherin the Mynde Is Styrred Paciently to Suffre all Afflictions Here* (1545) for distribution to her ladies. Four of the printed copies were bound in crimson velvet; she particularly favoured the daughter of Sir Brian Tuke, Master of the Posts, by presenting her with a manuscript version, written in girdle-book format: this survives, kept in the Mayor's Parlour at Kendal, Cumbria, where Catherine was born and where the family's ancestral lands were centred. Catherine's prayers were collected from a variety of sources, but the meditations themselves were taken from Thomas à Kempis's *Imitatio Christi*, that classic model of late-medieval affective spirituality, in the translation of Catherine of Aragon's spiritual advisor, the Syon monk Richard Whitford. There has been much discussion about Catherine's religious positioning in

124. Petrarch, *Canzoniere & Trionfi* (Venice, 1544). The covering is purple velvet; the embroidery, incoporating Catherine's arms, has been worked on linen and then applied. The supporters are a chained dog with fire issuing from its mouth on the dexter side and a wivern on the sinister. The British Library, C.27.e.19, cover

this work, but it is now generally agreed that she showed no clear religious alignment. She was, nevertheless, an unabashed promoter of the Gospel and certainly fashionably antipapal, comparing her husband to Moses and the pope to the Egyptian oppressor: 'But our Moyses, a moste godly, wise governer and kyng hath delivered us oute of the captivities and bondage of Pharao'. The analogy is not an unexpected or original one.

Although the inventory does not yield up much specific information about the actual constitution of Catherine's library, the little it does tell fits in with what is known about her character from other sources: the books are congruent with her image as a student of modern languages, with her reputation for learned piety and with her reformist fascination with scripture in the vernacular. According to John Foxe's account, the conservative bishop of Winchester, Stephen Gardiner, was instrumental in persuading Henry in 1546 that the queen harboured unorthodox religious views with alarming social implications – 'the religion by the Queen maintained did not only dissolve the politic government of princes, but also taught the people that all things ought to be in common' – and articles were drawn up for her arrest. These were based in part on forbidden reading matter she was alleged to possess: if the post-mortem collection is representative of the 'dangerous' books that were in her closet, then the charges must have been a total fabrication.

One of Catherine's great contributions was to bring the royal children together in their schooling: she herself oversaw the instruction of Edward and Elizabeth. She owned a copy of Robert Estienne's *Les mots françois selon l'ordre des lettres, ainsi que les fault escrire: tourner en latin, pour les enfans* (Paris, 1544), which has her name on the flyleaf and is now found in the British Library (C.28.f.3). The humanist scholar and provost of Eton, Nicholas Udall, commended above all her contribution to the Christian education of women in his preface to the translation of Erasmus's Paraphrase of St John:

> When I consider, most gracious Queen Katherine, the great number of noble women in this our time and country of England, not only given to the study of human sciences and of strange tongues, but also so thoroughly expert in Holy Scriptures, that they are able to compare with the best writers, as well in penning of godly and fruitful treatises to the instruction and edifying of the whole realm in the knowledge of God, as also in translating good books out of Latin or Greek into English for the use of such as are rude and ignorant of the said tongues, it is now no news at all to see queens and ladies of most high estate and progeny, instead of courtly dalliance, embrase virtuous exercises, reading and writing, and with most earnest study apply themselves to the acquiring of knowledge.

In Catherine's household, according to Udall, 'it is now a common thing to see young virgins so trained in the study of good letters that they willingly set all other vain pastimes at naught for learning's sake'. Fostered in this milieu, Princess Elizabeth produced for the queen's pleasure a French translation of Erasmus's *Dialogus fidei*, and she also undertook for her father a translation of Catherine's *Prayers or Meditations* into French, Latin and Italian; the dedicatory letter is dated 20 December 1545. (126) In 1544/5 she presented her step-dame with an English translation of the *Miroir de lame pecheresse*, a devotional tract by Marguerite of Navarre on the love of the soul for God and Christ – a fit tribute from the daughter of Anne Boleyn. (127) Catherine was also the force behind a project to translate Erasmus's Paraphrases of the Gospels into English under Udall's editorship. As Udall himself observed in his Paraphrase of St Luke, the queen was anxious to have devotional material of this sort distributed for the 'benefits of good English people now a long time sore thirsting and hungering the sincere and plaine knowledge of

125. According to these annotations a number of Catherine's books were delivered to Mary as queen.
The British Library,
Add. MS 46348, f. 208r

God's word'. Catherine's elder step-daughter, Princess Mary, undertook the
section on the Gospel of St John, but although the queen and Udall later
praised her proficiency – the former describing it as a 'fair and useful work'
– Mary was apparently too ill to complete her portion of the text.

One of the first things Mary did after she came to the throne was to take
possession of most of the books found in the inventory of Catherine's

goods, including the New Testaments in French and English. (125) Most scholars consider that these women stand at separate ends of the religious spectrum (reformist and traditional catholic), although it is acknowledged that there was a great affection between them. What this act of appropriation suggests, however, is that Mary saw her step-mother as a spiritual mentor as well as mediator with her fierce father and that she did not find her ideas as appalling as we might assume she would have done.

126. The presentation copy of Elizabeth's translation of Catherine's *Prayers or Meditations* has been bound in crimson silk binding, embroidered in gold and silver thread and coloured silks with the initial H, a large monogram of the name Katharina, and Tudor roses.
The British Library, Royal MS 7.D.x, cover

127. The cover of Elizabeth's translation into English of the *Miroir de lame pecheresse*, which may have been embroidered by the princess herself, consists of ornamental filigree work of silver and gold on a ground of blue corded silk with the initials K.P. in the middle of each cover.
Bodleian Library, Oxford, Cherry MS 36, cover

PART III:
SUBSEQUENT EVENTS

128–129. Located side by side at Westminster, where their inventory numbers were nos. 798 and 799, these two books have identical bindings by the London stationer John Reynes. Lambeth Palace Library, **H890.A51 & 1488.3, covers

During the protectorate of the young Edward VI's uncle, Edward Seymour, duke of Somerset, the Protestant Reformation became well and truly launched: Edward's brief reign saw, in the words of the Oxford historian Diarmaid MacCulloch, the triumph of the 'Tudor Church Militant'. In 1550, the Act against Superstitious Books and Images was passed, charging that

> all books called antiphoners, missals, grails, processionals, manuals, legends, pies, portuises, primers in Latin or English, couchers, ordinals, or other books or writings whatsoever heretofore used for the service of the Church, written or printed in the English or Latin tongue, other than such as are or shall be set forth by the King's Majesty, shall be by authority of this present Act clearly and utterly abolished, extinguished, and forbidden for ever to be used or kept in this realm or elsewhere within any of the King's dominions.

This was followed up in 1551 by an order in Council specifically naming the royal library:

> The Kinges Majesties lettre – for the purging of his Highnes Librarie at Westminster of all superstitiouse bookes, as masse bookes, legendes, and suche like, and to deliver the garnyture of the same bookes, being either of golde or silver, to Sir Anthony Aucher in the presence of Sir Thomas Darcie &c.

It is thus inevitable that few of the liturgical books described in the inventories of Henry's libraries still survive; presumably their destruction was accomplished under the willing supervision of the royal librarian Bartholomew Traheron, himself a Protestant of the most advanced views. Traheron also provided like-minded individuals such as John Bale with ancient manuscripts to be used to buttress the emerging 'Anglican' position by showing the uncontaminated state of the early, pre-Romish, church in England. A number of these manuscripts were taken abroad after Edward's death, at the time when the Marian exiles fled the country. Some formed the basis for scholarly editions issued in Basel and elsewhere – the manuscripts themselves subsequently used as printer's waste – and others quite possibly remain unidentified in continental collections even today.

Somerset himself received a copy of the first edition now in the Pierpont Morgan Library of 'a deuout treatyse in Englysshe, called the *Pylgrimage of Perfection*' 'from my Royale Maistere' and inscribed his name in it. Written by William Bonde, a brother of the Bridgettine house at Syon and intended especially for religious, the book has Henry's signature as well. It later passed, presumably through sequestration, to Mary, who has written 'Marye the quene / Ave Maria' on the table to the Third Book. It is precisely the sort

of text to have appealed to her religious sensibility and the Syon connection
would have made it doubly attractive.

During Mary's brief reign conservatives hoped that there would be a
concerted effort to retrieve monastic manuscripts from lay owners as part of
a campaign to restore the faith, if not the religious houses themselves. In
1556 John Dee, magus and scholar, composed 'A Supplication to Q. Mary...
for the recovery and preservation of ancient Writers and Monuments', in
which he proposed the establishment of a Library Royal and commissioners
who would go around the country looking for old books. Copies would be
made and the originals then restored to their present owners if they desired
them. Dee shrewdly recommended haste in this endeavour, since malicious
persons might otherwise hide the books in their possession. Even though
immensely sympathetic to a return to the pre-Reformation order, Mary did
not adopt Dee's scheme and it foundered, as would all similar proposals over
the next centuries.

Under Elizabeth many monastic books were further dispersed as the last
religious (some of whom had preserved collections in small underground
communities) gradually died off — but others were
recovered, on occasion from the very ruins of the
monasteries. Most went to private individuals but over
the course of the centuries many of these smaller collections have become absorbed into the royal (and ultimately the British) library. There were also attempts to
stabilize the library at Westminster and retrieve material which had strayed; in a letter to Matthew Parker,
for example, John Bale complained that Henry Fitza-
lan, earl of Arundel, had taken possession of the
unique copy of the *Historia Anglorum* by the medieval
St Albans chronicler Matthew Paris, and that this
should be returned: 'Chronica Matthaei Parys. Thys
chronycle remayneth in the custodye of my lorde of
Arundell, beynge a fayre boke, and written in an olde
latyne lettre. It belongeth to the quenes maiestyes
lybrary, lent by Bartylmew Trihearon such tyme as he had the kepynge of that
lybrarye in kynge Edwardes tyme.' (130) Under the librarians who succeeded
Traheron, John Cliffe, Anthony Martin, Andrew Bright, and Edmund
Doubleday, Elizabeth gave away selected items to her cronies, including her
former tutor and cousin Sir John Fortescue. During this period Sir Thomas
Knyvett (1545–1622), groom of the Privy Chamber and keeper of Whitehall,
presided over things and seems to have permitted extensive depredations. In
1605, nevertheless, when Sir Thomas Bodley got a warrant from King James
I 'for the choice of any books that I shall like in any of his houses of librarys'
Knyvett and Sir Peter Young, James's former tutor, managed to have it rescin-
ded. As a result Bodley acquired nothing directly from this source, although a
number of royal books did ultimately end up at Oxford. This thwarting of
Bodley also signalled a new movement towards preservation, albeit preservation in a more flexible sense than modern curators interpret the term.

130. After the conclusion of the
autograph copy of the *Historia
Anglorum* an image of the death
of the author, Matthew Paris, has
been added. This is a significant
manuscript, in part because it
contains annotations by the sixteenth-century Italian humanist
and (not altogether sympathetic)
chronicler of English history,
Polydore Vergil.
The British Library,
Royal MS 14.C.VII, f. 218v

Soon after Bodley's unsuccessful assault on the library, Sir Peter's fifth son, Patrick (d. 1652), took charge and was commissioned to make a cata‚ logue, but Knyvett initially refused to surrender the keys to him, and this led to a bitter exchange of letters. Presumably, too, it was Knyvett who permit‚ ted Richard Bancroft, archbishop of Canterbury, to take possession of books. In December 1610, shortly after Bancroft's death, Young – by this point officially keeper of the king's libraries – wrote to James Montagu, bishop of Bath and Wells, complaining that the archbishop had borrowed at least five hundred volumes – and for the period this was a staggering number – from the royal collection. Some Bancroft had returned, according to Young, but the majority had been bound and stamped with his own arms, and had been entered in his catalogues. Bancroft left his own collec‚ tion of six thousand and sixty‚five books, of which three hundred and fifty‚ two were manuscripts, for the establishment of an archiepiscopal library at Lambeth and most of the books can still be found *in situ*. Several of the manuscripts have indications of earlier royal provenance, as do a consider‚ able number of the printed books; indeed the Bancroft cache represents the largest single group of Henrician books outside the British Library. It is an important group, too, because almost all the books are in their original bind‚ ings and this gives a good sense of how sections of the Westminster library might have looked by the end of Henry's reign. (128–129)

Although Young attempted to retrieve some borrowed books, he gave others away to friends and colleagues. Montagu, to whom Young com‚ plained about Bancroft in 1610, was the first master of Sidney Sussex Col‚ lege Cambridge, as well as bishop of Bath and Wells. When he died in 1630, Montagu left all his books to Sidney Sussex College: among these are two Henrician books which he acquired from Young, in concert with whom he had edited and translated writings by King James. (131) James Ussher (1581–1656), archbishop of Armagh, and virtual founder of the library at Trinity College Dublin, also had access to Henrician books and obtained an important illuminated manuscript from Winchcombe, a twelfth‚century psalter – 'bellissime scriptum' as it was described in the Westminster inventory – containing miniatures of the very highest quality. It is not impossible that it is one of the unnamed books the abbot of Winch‚ combe sent to Cromwell in 1535, perhaps even selected by Henry himself after he and Anne Boleyn visited the monastery on their royal progress in that year. (132)

Young's dealings with the most famous of the seventeenth‚century anti‚ quaries, Sir Robert Cotton (1571–1631), were complex and involved a number of manuscript exchanges. One of the items obtained by Cotton is an illuminated manuscript from the early fifteenth century made up of two treatises: the Middle English version of William Twiti's *The Art of Hunting* – a handbook which set out the etiquette of the hunt as well as giving hunt‚ ing lore – and Edward Plantagenet, second duke of York's *The Master of Game*, which bears witness, like *Sir Gawain and the Green Knight*, to the com‚ plex rituals surrounding the aristocratic hunt. (133) Presumably this is a book which Henry inherited from one of his ancestors; certainly it was not

131. *Above left* Henry was responsible for
the publication of this Protestation against
the General Council which Pope Paul III
summoned for Mantua in 1537. It is just the
sort of book that would have appealed to
Montagu. The inventory number, no. 776,
is just visible in spite of cropping.
By permission of the Master and Fellows of Sidney Sussex
College, Cambridge, Bb.6.7(2), title page

132. *Above right* The image of David as harpist
would have appealed to Henry, who saw the
psalmist as one of his biblical prototypes. This
initial from the Winchcombe Psalter contains
lion masks, imaginary beasts and figures playing
instruments.
The Board of Trinity College Dublin, MS 53, f. 151

133. *Left* The opening leaf of *The Art of
Hunting*, to which no. 373 has been appended,
illustrates the various quarries in their natural
habitats.
The British Library, Cotton MS Vespasian B.xii, f. 31

a monastic trophy. Why Cotton wanted it is not altogether clear, although he did have a higher regard for books in the vernacular than most of his contemporaries, acquiring, for example, the unique copy of *Beowulf* as well as the Gawain manuscript.

Young kept up his Scottish connections after he came south and one of the most beautiful of the Westminster books to migrate elsewhere is the so-called Aberdeen Bestiary which had come to the royal library from an unknown English monastery before 1542. (137). It forms part of a bequest of approximately one thousand three hundred and fifty books and manuscripts to Marischal College Library at Aberdeen University by Thomas Reid, Latin secretary to James I from 1618 until his death in 1624. Like Montagu, Reid was associated with Young in the translation of James's writings and Young rewarded him with this manuscript as well as with several others which had been inherited from Lord Lumley's library by the unfortunate Prince Henry, who died in 1612. Lumley, in turn, got his core collection from his father-in-law, Arundel, who, as we have seen, is known to have taken possession of Henrician books.

According to the so-called Foundation List of 1612–13 Young presented eight items – most deriving from the royal library – to the University of St Andrews, from which he graduated MA in 1603. Appropriately one of these was the immensely learned and influential Complutensian polyglot Bible. Yet another Scottish recipient of Young's largesse was Sir James Balfour of Denmilne and Kinnaird (1600–57) who travelled to London in 1628 to study heraldry. He returned to Scotland in 1630, was made Lyon king-of-arms and was knighted by Charles I in the same year. A devoted antiquary, he had a fine collection of manuscripts which was bought in 1698 by the Faculty of Advocates, becoming part of National Library of Scotland in 1925. It was Balfour's practice to note the date on which he acquired books and four of those he obtained during his time in London come from the Westminster collection.

Pope Clement VII sent Henry a copy of Francesco Giorgi's *De harmonia mundi* ('On the Harmony of the Universe'), a mystical work partially deriving from the Hebrew Cabbalah, and it is extensively annotated. In 1640, the year the Long Parliament was called, it was sold from the royal collection, but there is no evidence that Young was responsible for the sale. (134) Even if he did not sell books, Young did, however, lend them and they were not always returned. In a document dated to 19 August 1646, for example, he testified:

> Where as I Patricke Young Gentleman, Keeper of his Maiesties Library, did diverse yeares since lend unto Sir Henry Spelman Knight one Ancient Manuscript in a large 4° bound in course blacke velvet with bosses and claspes guilded, containing in it amongst other particulars divers of the old English Saxon Lawes in Latine, I doe now declare the booke lately lent unto Sir Simonds D'Ewes by the Lady Spelman which I have seen in his custody is the same booke, which I lent unto the said Sir Henry Spelman being one of the bookes belonging to his Majesties Library.

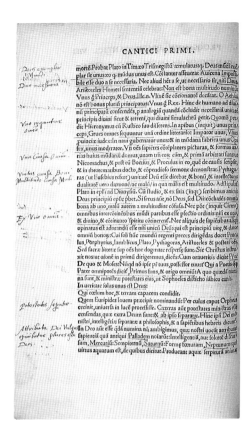
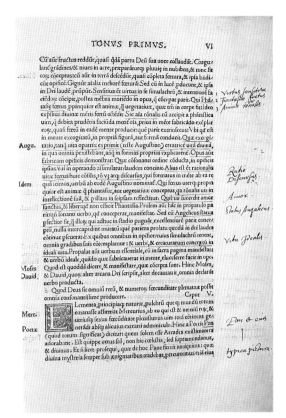

The binding is characteristic of Henrician books and Young's statement also shows the fluid state of collections during the turbulent times of the Interregnum. When he witnessed to this loss Young's own position was at risk as a result of the Civil War and he felt under siege. By early 1649, the year of Charles I's execution, his keepership had come to an end and there was some talk of selling off the royal library to foreign buyers. Later in that year, however, it was decided that the books should be preserved and that an inventory be prepared. Young was assigned this task and on 20 November 1650 he announced that only a few had gone missing, although one of the most desirable – the Psalter of Queen Ingeburg, now at the Chantilly Museum, presented to Mary Tudor by Phillip of Spain at the time of their marriage – was among them.

When Young retired from the royal library he was permitted to take away with him the Codex Alexandrinus – a fifth-century copy of the Greek Bible given to King James by the former patriarch of Alexandria – as well as other unidentified books. (He was a considerable scholar and, like Leland, intended to produce editions from the texts he discovered in ancient codices.) After his death the books were not returned and on 28 September 1652 the Council of State set about retrieving them. In spite of the efforts of the Council, so it appears, the books remained with Young's heirs throughout

134. Giorgi, who dedicated this book to Clement, later supported Henry's position concerning the (in)validity of his first marriage.

Reproduced by permission of the Master and Fellows of Emmanuel College, Cambridge, MSS 3.1.44, f. 36

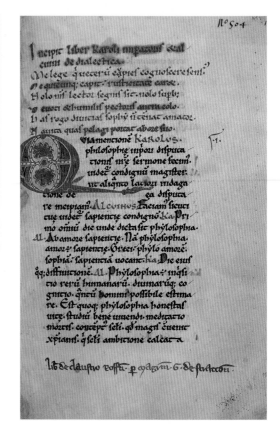

135. *Left* *Le mortifiement de vaine*
plaisance is the one religious piece
by René d'Anjou (1409–80),
king of Naples and Jerusalem.
It is a dialogue carried on by
allegorical figures concerning the
love of God as the way to purge
the soul of all earthly folly.
Bodleian Library, Oxford,
Cherry MS 4, f. 9r

136. *Right* This early twelfth-
century manuscript of the *De*
dialectica by the Anglo-Saxon
scholar and monk Alcuin is one
of eight Henrician manuscripts
found at Trinity College
Cambridge. The characteristic
inventory number, no. 504, is
found on the first leaf.
The Master and Fellows of Trinity
College, Cambridge, MS O. 2. 24, f. 1r

the Commonwealth. With the Restoration a new offensive was launched
and on 9 February 1664 Young's son-in-law, John Atwood, was required to
deliver to Thomas Ross, Keeper of the King's Library, sixty-seven folio and
fifty quarto and octavo manuscripts as well as an assortment of printed
books belonging to the royal library. Atwood responded to the demand on
5 March, stating that he had examined the books in his possession and
found three Latin works with Lord Lumley's name in them but none with
the king's arms or mark. (Obviously Atwood suppressed all knowledge – if
he had such – of the significance of the Westminster inventory number.)
Atwood must have returned the Codex Alexandrinus to the royal library,
since that is where it is now found, but others did not go back, such as two
items given by Young's grandson Leigh Atwood to the nonjuror Francis
Cherry (?1665–1713), and now found in the Bodleian Library. (135) A
number went from Young's heirs to John Owen (1616–83), dean of Christ-
church and thence, via the antiquary Thomas Gale (d. 1702) and his son
Roger (d. 1744), to Trinity College Cambridge. (136) As a result Trinity
has the single largest cache of Henrician manuscripts, if not printed books,
outside the British Library.

137. In this illustration of Adam naming the Beasts in the Aberdeen Bestiary the animals, evenly distributed over the page, move towards him. University of Aberdeen Library, MS 24, f. 5r

CONCLUSION

IN RECENT YEARS the history of the book has become a recognized academic discipline and more and more scholars have used the physical evidence books offer us – both through text and marginalia – as a means of engaging in a living dialogue with the past. Nowadays, then, most scholars take it as virtually axiomatic that institutional collections should be kept intact. As we have seen, this is a very recent point of view and during the period before the Civil War the royal collection suffered both losses and reconfigurations – i.e. some manuscripts were dismembered and reassembled in different order, with deletions or added sections, to produce quite different meanings through new contexts. Antiquaries such as Cotton and Young had their own political agendas and they sometimes manipulated manuscripts to reflect their views; the past, in the form of medieval manuscripts, could thus be reshaped in accordance with their views of what it should have been. On other occasions it is impossible to ascertain the reasons for their dismemberings. (138) Only in the eighteenth century was there a reaction against this sort of practice, the scholar librarian Humphrey Wanley roundly condemning the earlier collector Sir Simonds D'Ewes (whom we have already encountered as a receiver of purloined royal books):

> It seemeth a little extraordinary to me that Sir Simonds D'Ewes should … take his old Book, and cutt off the first leaf or leaves; rase off the 3 first lines in another place wherein were the conclusion of a former Chapter, & the Title of the next; write thereon a new Title for the Book … and that he should, to crown the matter, prefix a new Fronstispiece or Title of his own Invention thereunto, to make the World believe that this was not to be deemed a book of that Kind that it proveth to be. *Query* Whether it be fair for any Gentleman to do these things by an old History, although the Book be his own Property.

All of us would respond to Wanley's enquiry with a resounding negative. In Leland's generation the question would not even have made sense.

Unlike many others, Henry's manuscript collection has remained a relatively well-preserved one: in spite of seven moves between 1697/8, when Whitehall was destroyed by fire, and the final arrival of the codices at Montagu House in 1759, few manuscripts disappeared after the Restoration. Some were, nevertheless, damaged in another fire in 1731 and at least one, a thirteenth-century Bestiary in French, was stolen in the nineteenth century. Since then there have been no losses, not even during the Second World War. Whether or not the current pressures to restore treasures, such as the Lindisfarne Gospels, to their earlier environments will change this state of affairs remains to be seen.

The fate of the printed books has been less happy, primarily because of a series of eight duplicate sales held between 1769 and 1832. This has led to wide dissemination: one book with a Westminster inventory number which was sold in 1769 is now in Geneva and another is in Antwerp; one from the sale of 1788 is in the National Library of Scotland; some are in Paris and others untraced. Three have migrated to Windsor, which perhaps represents a kind of 'royal' homecoming. (139) At least one Henrician book from the British Museum stock was destroyed by German bombing during the Second World War – at Lambeth, alas, there were many more casualties.

Our continuing fascination with Henry's reign is not simply a result of the soap opera surrounding his private life: rather it is because these years witnessed the transformation of English religious life, the birth of a new

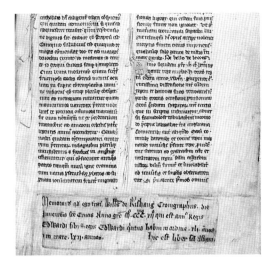

138. This autobiographical memorandum identifying the medieval chronicler of St Albans, William Rishanger, was originally found in the lower margin of the opening page of the Account of the Barons' War of 1263–67. In the seventeenth century it was excised by either Cotton or Young and was glued on to the first folio of another booklet, which had no association with Rishanger. The motivation for this cannot be determined. Sir Frederic Madden, head of the manuscripts department in the British Museum from 1837, restored it to its original place.
The British Library, Cotton MS Claudius D.VI, f. 101r

139. This copy in low German of *Dat boek des hyllighen Ewangelii Profecien und Epistelen* was sold as a duplicate. Subsequently owned by William Morris and C. Fairfax Murray, it was bought for Windsor for £120 in 1929. On the title page is inscribed 'Henry is my best freind'.
The Royal Collection © 2004, Her Majesty Queen Elizabeth II, RL III 67 I, title page

state church, the acquisition of the estates of the dissolved monasteries by powerful Tudor families – the Pagets, Cecils, Wriothesleys, Russells, Thynnes, Horners and Wyndhams. In some sense, too, our educational system, from top to bottom, had to be rethought after the monasteries fell and the local choir schools disappeared. During Henry's reign it became clear that the printing press was going to triumph over manuscript culture, and the modern institutional library as we know it began to take shape. Central to the understanding of all these phenomena is the book in one form or another: Henry's collection is a great treasure-house, intellectually and aesthetically, one which still has much to reveal.

This book grows out of *The Libraries of King Henry VIII* (Corpus of British Medieval Library Catalogues 7; London: 2000), which gives fuller information on many of the manuscripts and printed books to which I make allusion here. In some sense *The Libraries* is a companion volume to this and provides a bibliographical context which is not repeated here: the sources for many of my quotations, for example, are found in it. A large proportion of Henry's manuscripts came from dissolved monasteries, moreover, and a goodly number are listed in other volumes in the Corpus series. A description of the cataloguing systems in Henry's libraries is found in my 'Marks in Books and the Libraries of Henry VIII', *Papers of the Bibliographical Society of America* 91 (1997), 583–606. There is a further discussion in my 'The Royal Library under Henry VIII', in *The Cambridge History of the Book in Britain, III: 1400–1557*, edited by Lotte Hellinga and J. B. Trapp (Cambridge, 1999), pp. 274–81. Maria Hayward has edited *The 1542 Inventory of Whitehall*, 2 vols (London, 2004), and *The Inventory of King Henry VIII: The Transcript* edited by David Starkey (London, 1998) lists almost 20,000 items, including books, possessed by the king at the time of his death.

The Survey of Manuscripts Illuminated in the British Isles series issued in six volumes under the general editorship of J. J. G. Alexander is an important guide to illuminated manuscripts, some of which figure in my discussions, from the sixth century until 1490. Other manuscripts to which I refer, especially in my chapter on inherited books, feature in Janet Backhouse's *The Illuminated Page: Ten Centuries of Manuscript Painting in the British Library* (London, 1997). The best general survey of bookbinding is H. M. Nixon and M. M. Foot, *The History of Decorated Bookbinding in England* (Oxford, 1992): it provides references to specialized studies of individual binders. The definitive account on the transition from manuscript to print is Elizabeth L. Eisenstein's *The Printing Press as an Agent of Change* (Cambridge, 1979). Pamela Neville-Sington examines 'Press, politics and religion', in *The Cambridge History of the Book in Britain, III*, pp. 576–607. Christopher de Hamel charts the development of biblical codices throughout the Middle Ages and into the era of print in *The Book: A History of the Bible* (New York, 2001). Francis M. Higman has undertaken a full bibliographical analysis of *Piety and the People: Religious Printing in French 1511–1551* (Aldershot, 1996).

The standard account of Henry VIII's reign remains J. J. Scarisbrick's *Henry VIII* (London, 1968). Official documents are calendared in *Letters and Papers, Foreign and Domestic, of the Reign of Henry VIII*, edited by J. S. Brewer et al., 21 vols in 33 and addenda (London, 1862–1932). Simon Thurley examines the physical setting in *The Royal Palaces of Tudor England* (New Haven and London, 1993) and the wider cultural milieu is covered in *Henry VIII: A European Court in England*, edited by David Starkey (London, 1991). More generally see *The History of the King's Works*, edited by H. M. Colvin et al., 6 vols (London, 1963–82). There are brief biographies of many of my *dramatis personae* in *Contemporaries of Erasmus*, edited by P. Bietenholz, 3 vols (Toronto, 1985–7). A number of these individuals are also mentioned in James K. McConica's *English Humanists and Reformation Politics under Henry VIII and Edward VI* (Oxford, 1965). The quotations from Erasmus are in the translations of the Collected Works of Erasmus in English series published by the University of Toronto Press and can readily be located there. Richard Sharpe's *Handlist of the Latin Writers of Great Britain and Ireland Before 1540* (Brepols, 1997) is a rich source of information on modern editions of individual writers' works and the manuscripts in which these are found.

Introduction

Glenn Richardson's *Renaissance Monarchy. The Reigns of Henry VIII, Francis I and Charles V* (London, 2002) puts Henry's reign in a wider context. R. J. Knecht, *Renaissance Warrior and Patron: The Reign of Francis I* (Cambridge, 1994), pp. 471–7, gives a very useful account of Francis I's library, as does J. Cox-Rearick in *The Collection of Francis I: Royal Treasures* (New York, 1996), pp. 368–72. T. Kimball Brooker looks at 'Bindings Commissioned for Francis I's "Italian Library" with Horizontal Spine Titles Dating from the Late 1530s to 1540', in *Bulletin du bibliophile* 1997, no. 1, 33–91. M. D. Orth has made an exhaustive *Survey of French Renaissance Illuminated Manuscripts 1515–1570* (London and Turnhout, forthcoming). Orth and I have examined 'Simon Bourgouyn and his French Translations from Plutarch, Petrarch and Lucian', in *Viator* 34 (2003), 328–63 and have made a comparative survey of the function of translation at the French and English court.

The Aristotelian concept of magnificence in Tudor England is examined by Gordon Kipling in *The Triumph of Honour: Burgundian Origins of the English Renaissance* (The Hague, 1977) and by Sydney Anglo in *Images of Tudor Kingship* (London, 1992). J. N. King's *Tudor Royal Iconography* (Princeton, N.J., 1989) is also useful. The unpublished Latin poem by Sir Thomas More survives in BL MS Cotton Titus D.iv; the quote from Erasmus comes from Epistle 964 and that from Mountjoy from Epistle 215. Richard Pace's *De Fructu qui ex Doctrina Percipitur* has been edited and translated by Frank Manley and Richard S. Sylvester (New York, 1967). Wouter Deleen's career is examined by J. Trapman in 'Delenus en de bijbel', *Nederlands archief voor kerkgeschiednis* 56 (1975), 95–113. On Marler's Great Bible see T. C. String, 'Henry VIII's Illuminated "Great Bible"', *The Journal of the Warburg and Courtauld Institutes* 59 (1996), 315–24.

Chapter 1: The Physical Setting

Maria Hayward describes 'The Packing and Transportation of the Possessions of Henry VIII, with Particular Reference to the 1547 Inventory', in *Costume* 31 (1997), 8–15. Janet Backhouse discusses girdle-books in 'Illuminated Manuscripts and the Early Development of the Portrait Miniature', in *Early Tudor England: Proceedings of the 1987 Harlaxton Symposium*, edited by D. Williams (Woodbridge, 1989), 1–17. Hugh Tait treats the same theme in 'The Girdle-prayerbook or "Tablett": an Important Class of Renaissance Jewellery at the Court of Henry VIII', in *Jewellery Studies* 2 (1985), 29–57. The inventories of the Henrician libraries have been edited and analysed in my *The Libraries of King Henry VIII*, where full references to

Waldstein and the duke of Stettin-Pomerania are provided.
Further analysis of the Greenwich collection is found in my
'Greenwich and Henry VIII's Royal Library' (*Henry VIII*,
edited by Starkey, pp. 155–59). Alan Coates describes
Thomas Pope's benefaction in 'The Old Library of Trinity
College, Oxford', *Bodleian Library Record* 13 (1991), 470–77
and in *The Old Library Trinity College, Oxford* (Oxford, 1988),
edited by Richard Gameson and A. Coates, pp. 9–11, 50–51.

A facsimile of Henry's French chansonnier has been pro-
duced by H. M. Brown for *Renaissance Music in Facsimile* 2
(New York and London, 1988). The *Assertio septem sacra-
mentorum aduersus Martinum Lutherum* has been edited by Pierre
Fraenkel (Münster, 1992) and the *Grauissimae atque exactissimae
illustrissimarum totius Italiae et Galliae academiarum censurae* by
Edward Surtz and Virginia Murphy (Angers, 1988).
The letter by Niccolò Sagudino, secretary to the Venetian
ambassador, Sebastiano Giustiniani, in 1515 is printed in
Four Years at the Court of Henry VIII: [1515–1519], trans.
Rawdon Brown (London, 1854), 1.76, 79.

Chapter 2: Inherited Books

Although very few lists of books associated with English
monarchs before Henry VIII survive, Jenny Stratford has
given a summary of the evidence in 'The Royal Library in
England Before the Reign of Edward IV', in *England in the
Fifteenth Century: Proceedings of the 1992 Harlaxton Symposium*,
edited by N. Rogers (Stamford, 1994), pp. 187–97. There is
no comprehensive survey of royal books from the English
Middle Ages, but a variety of documents have been examined by R. F. Green in *Poets and Princepleasers: Literature and
the English Court in the Late Middle Ages* (Toronto, 1980), pp.
91–100, 140–45; J. J. G. Alexander, 'Painting and
Manuscript Illumination for Royal Patrons in the Later
Middle Ages', in *English Court Culture in the Later Middle
Ages*, edited by V. J. Scattergood and J. W. Sherborne
(London, 1983), pp. 141–62; A. I. Doyle, 'English Books
In and Out of Court from Edward III to Henry VI', ibid.
pp. 163–81; J. J. G. Alexander, 'Foreign Illuminators and
Illuminated Manuscripts', in *The Cambridge History of the
Book in Britain, III*, edited by Hellinga and Trapp, pp. 47–64;
J. Stratford, 'The Early Royal Collections and the Royal
Library to 1461', ibid. pp. 255–66; J. M. Backhouse, 'The
Royal Library from Edward IV to Henry VII', ibid.
267–73; Thomas Kren and Scot McKendrick, *Illuminating
the Renaissance* (Los Angeles and London, 2003); and my
'The Royal Library under Henry VIII', ibid. pp. 274–81.

Richard II's books are the focus of R. F. Green's 'King
Richard II's Books Revisited', *The Library* 31 (1976),
235–39. Lucy F. Sandler writes about books owned by the
Bohun family in 'A Note on the Illuminators of the Bohun
Manuscripts', *Speculum* 60 (1985), 364–72. She has studied
books associated with the Bohuns elsewhere and has a recent
essay, for example, on 'Political Imagery in the Bohun
Manuscripts', in *English Manuscript Studies* 10 (2002), 114–53.
Jeanne Krochalis describes 'The Books and Reading of
Henry V and His Circle', in *The Chaucer Review* 23 (1988),
50–77. Duke Humfrey's books have been studied by
Alfonso Sammut in his *Unfredo Duca di Gloucester e gli
Umanisti Italiani* (Padua, 1980). Further materials relating to
Humfrey as a book collector are coming to light in a series of
essays being written by David Rundle. Kathleen Scott

includes the presentation copy of John Lydgate's Life of
Sts Edmund and Fremund in her *Later Gothic Manuscripts
1390–1490, A Survey of Manuscripts Illuminated in the
British Isles* 6, gen. edited by J. J. G. Alexander, 2 vols.
(London, 1996), no. 78. Anne F. Sutton and Livia Visser
Fuchs have published articles on Richard III's books and
these have been brought together and supplemented in their
Richard III's Books (Stroud, 1997). The authoritative study of
Edward IV's books is Janet Backhouse's 'Founders of the
Royal Library: Edward IV and Henry VII as Collectors of
Illuminated Manucripts', in *England in the Fifteenth Century:
Proceedings of the 1986 Harlaxton Symposium*, edited by Daniel
Williams (Woodbridge, 1987), pp. 23–41. Individual man-
uscripts have been examined by Scot McKendrick, in '*La
Grande Histoire Cesar* and the Manuscripts of Edward IV',
English Manuscript Studies 1100–1700 2 (1990), 109–138; in
'Lodewijk van Gruuthuse en de Librije van Edward IV', in
Lodewijk van Gruuthuse, edited by M. P. J. Martens (Bruges,
1992), 153–59; and in 'The *Romuléon* and the Manuscripts
of Edward IV', in *England in the Fifteenth Century. Proceedings
of the 1992 Harlaxton Symposium*, edited by Nicholas Rogers
(Stamford, 1994), 149–69. Backhouse analyses 'Illuminated
Manuscripts Associated with Henry VII and Members of
his Immediate Family', in *The Reign of Henry VII: Proceedings
of the 1993 Harlaxton Symposium*, edited by Benjamin
Thompson (Stamford, 1995), pp. 175–87. Paul Gwynne
discusses Johannes Michael Nagonius's manuscript in
'The Frontispiece to an Illuminated Panegyric of Henry VII:
A Note on the Sources', *Journal of the Warburg and Courtauld
Institutes* 55 (1992), 266–70; and David R. Carlson looks
at the politics behind Johannes Opicius's gift of poems to
Henry in 'The "Opicius" poems (British Library, Cotton
Vespasian B.iv) and the Humanist Anti-literature in
Early Tudor England', *Renaissance Quarterly* 55 (2002),
869–904. Opicius has also been the focus of two articles
by L. Wahlgren-Smith: 'Heraldry in Arcadia: the Court
Eclogue of Johannes Opicius', *Renaissance Studies* 14 (2000),
210–34; and 'An Early Tudor Political Pastoral: The
Dialogus of Johannes Opicius', in *Tongues and Texts Unlimited*,
ed. H. Aili and P. af Trampe Stockholm, 2000), pp. 243–60.
Mary Hamel identifies books inherited from Cecily Welles
in 'Arthurian Romance in Fifteenth-Century Lindsey: The
Books of the Lords Welles', *Modern Language Quarterly* 51
(1990), 341–61. Mary Beth Winn has examined the printed
books acquired by Henry VII from Antoine Vérard in her
comprehensive study of *Anthoine Vérard, Parisian Publisher,
1485–1512: Prologues, Poems, and Presentations* (Geneva, 1997).
She has also provided me with references to further examples
which have come to light since 1997, including the *Jardin de
santé* in Kentucky. Lady Margaret Beaufort's books are mentioned in Michael K. Jones and Malcolm G. Underwood's
*The King's Mother: Lady Margaret Beaufort, Countess of Richmond
and Derby* (Cambridge, 1992); they are more closely analysed
by Sue Powell in 'Lady Margaret and Her Books', *The
Library*, 6th ser. 20 (1998), 197–240.

Chapter 3: New Year's Gifts and Other Presentations

In my 'Henry VIII's Library and Humanist Donors: Gian
Matteo Giberti as Case Study', *Reassessing Tudor Humanism*,
edited by Jonathan Woolfson (New York, 2002), pp. 99–128)
I discuss the types of books received by Henry and contexts

in which they were given. David. R. Carlson gives an excellent general survey of *English Humanist Books: Writers and Patrons, Manuscript and Print 1475–1525* (Toronto, 1993), and J. B. Trapp specifically concerns himself with *Erasmus, Colet and More: The Early Tudor Humanists and Their Books* (London, 1991). Carlson has written on 'The Occasional Poetry of Pietro Carmeliano', in *Aevum* 61 (1987), 495–502, and on 'The Writings of Bernard André (*c.* 1450–*c.* 1522)', in *Renaissance Studies* 12 (1998), 229–50. Pieter Meghen has been the focus of three articles by J. B. Trapp: 'Notes on Manuscripts Written by Peter Meghen', *The Book Collector* 24 (1975), 80–96; 'Pieter Meghen 1466/7 1540, Scribe and Courier', *Erasmus in English* 11 (1981/2), 28–35; 'Pieter Meghen, Yet Again', *Manuscripts in the Fifty Years After the Invention of Printing*, edited by J. B. Trapp (London, 1983), pp. 23–8. The book now at Charlecote Park was described by Cecil H. Clough in 'A Presentation Volume for Henry VIII: The Charlecote Park Copy of Erasmus's *Institutio principis Christiani*', *Journal of the Warburg and Courtauld Institutes* 44 (1981), 199–202. Richard Cooper has written on 'Jean Mallard, poète et peintre rouennais', in *Première poésie française de la Renaissance: autour des Puys poétiques normands*, edited by J.-C Arnould and T. Mantovani (Paris, 2003), pp. 193–213. The iconography of Henry's Psalter is discussed by Pamela Tudor-Craig, 'Henry VIII and King David', in *Early Tudor England,* edited by Williams, pp. 183–205; and by John N. King in 'Henry VIII as David: the King's Image and Reformation Politics', in *Rethinking the Henrician Era*, edited by P. C. Herman (Urbana and Chicago, 1994), pp. 78–92. Helen Wallis has produced a facsimile edition of *The Maps and Text of the Boke of Idrography Presented by Jean Rotz to Henry VIII* (Oxford, 1981). There is a short note by Margaret Rogerson on 'Robert/Ralph Radcliffe: A Case of Mistaken Identity', in *Notes and Queries* 245 (2000), 23–26. *'Triumphs of English': Henry Parker, Lord Morley, Translator to the Tudor Court*, edited by M. Axton and J. P. Carley (London, 2000), provides an examination of the career of Lord Morley from a variety of perspectives. The original layout and decoration of the Greek Genesis has been lovingly reconstructed from the burned fragments by K. Weitzmann and H. L. Kessler, *The Cotton Genesis* (Princeton, 1986). I discuss the manner in which it came to Henry in 'Thomas Wakefield, Robert Wakefield and the Cotton Genesis', *Transactions of the Cambridge Bibliographical Society* 12.3 (2002), 246–261. David S. Berkowitz includes the Golden Gospels in his catalogue *In Remembrance of Creation* (Waltham, Mass., 1968), no. 58. The account of Pierfrancesco di Piero Bardi's association with Henry is a summary of my 'Religious Controversy and Marginalia: Pierfrancesco di Piero Bardi, Thomas Wakefield and their Books', *Transactions of the Cambridge Bibliographical Society* 12.3 (2002), 206–45. Shelley Lockwood has given an excellent description of the ways in which William Marshall manipulated his sources in 'Marsilius of Padua and the Case for the Royal Ecclesiastical Supremacy', *Transactions of the Royal Historical Society*, 6th ser. 1 (1991), 89–119. Giacomo Calco is treated more fully in my 'Misattributions and Ghost Entries in John Bale's *Index Britanniae Scriptorum*', in *Anglo-Latin and Its Heritage*, edited by S. Echard and G. R. Wieland (Turnhout, 2001), pp. 229–42. Joyce Boro will touch upon the literary career of John Bourchier, Lord Berners, in her forthcoming edition of *The Castell of Love*. Janet Backhouse

and I consider his relationship with the Beddington books in an essay which will appear in volume 2 of *The Inventory of King Henry VIII*.

Chapter 4: Sequestrations

Peter Gwyn's full-scale biography of *The King's Cardinal: The Rise and Fall of Thomas Wolsey* (London, 1990) does not, in fact, deal with Wolsey's books as such. I discuss the TC monogram in 'Sir Thomas Bodley's Library and Its Acquisitions: An Edition of the Nottingham Benefaction of 1604', in *Books and Collectors 1200–1700: Essays Presented to Andrew Watson*, edited by J. P. Carley and C. G. C. Tite (London, 1997), pp. 359–60; also in 'Marks in Books and the Libraries of Henry VIII', *The Papers of the Bibliographical Society of America* 91 (1997), 597–8. Although much has been written about the use of biblical sources in the King's 'Great Matter', the importance of the commentaries gathered in from the monastic houses seems to gone virtually unnoticed until recently, no less a scholar than N. R. Ker enquiring: 'I have wondered what the king, or whoever was responsible for his library, wanted with four copies of Ralph of Flavigny on Leviticus': 'The Migration of Manuscripts from the English Medieval Libraries', repr. from *The Library*, 4th ser. 23 (1942–3), 1–11 in his *Books, Collectors and Libraries*, edited by Andrew G. Watson (London and Ronceverte, 1985), p. 467. Linacre's presentation manuscripts to Henry and Wolsey have been catalogued by Giles Barber in 'Thomas Linacre: A Bibliographical Survey of His Works', in *Essays on the Life and Work of Thomas Linacre c.1460–1524*, edited by F. Maddison, M. Pelling and C. Webster (Oxford, 1977), pp. 290–336. Carlson compares the printed version of Robert Whittinton's *Opusculum* with the 'reduplicated' copy presented to Wolsey and examines the motives for this gesture in *English Humanist Books*, ch. 5. As the late Sir Geoffrey Elton showed so lucidly, Thomas Cromwell played a key role in Henry's government throughout the 1530s and John Guy charts the relationship of his policies to those of his predecessor as chief minister in 'Thomas Wolsey, Thomas Cromwell and the Reform of Henrician Government', in *The Reign of Henry VIII: Politics, Policy and Piety*, edited by Diarmaid MacCulloch (Basingstoke and London, 1995), pp. 35–57. To date, however, there have been only two articles devoted to his books as such: L. A. Sheppard, 'A Vellum Copy of the "Great Bible," 1539', *The National Library of Wales Journal* 1 (1939–40), 9–22; and my '"Plutrach's" Life of Agesilaus: A Recently Located New Year's Gift to Thomas Cromwell by Henry Parker, Lord Morley', in *Prestige, Authority and Power in Late Medieval Manuscripts and Texts*, edited by Felicity Riddy (Woodbridge, 2000), pp. 159–69. Maria Dowling looks at John Fisher's library in her biography *Fisher of Men: A Life of John Fisher, 1469–1535* (London and New York 1999); in her view Cromwell's cronies would have received many of the books, although not the medieval manuscripts, which were sent to the royal library. I first hypothesized that large numbers of medieval manuscripts from Rochester got to the royal library at the time of Fisher's fall in 'John Leland and the Foundations of the Royal Library: The Westminster Inventory of 1542', *Bulletin of the Society for Renaissance Studies* 7 (1989), 13–22 (p. 19). In 'John Leland and the Contents of English Pre-Dissolution Libraries: Lincolnshire', *Transactions of the*

Cambridge Bibliographical Society 9.4 (1989), 330–57 I showed why the list of books in Royal Appendix 69 could not have been compiled by Leland and why it must have been drawn up around 1530. R. W. Hoyle has delved into 'The Origins of the Dissolution of the Monasteries', in *The Historical Journal* 38.2 (1995), 275–305. In his commentary to Leland's New Year's gift, which he printed as *The Laboryouse Journey & Serche of John Leylande, for Englandes Antiquitees Geven of Hym as a New Yeares gyfte to Kynge Henry the VIII. in the XXXVII. Yeare of his Reygne, with Declaratyons Enlarged by Johan Bale* (London, 1549; repr. Norwood, N.J. and Amsterdam, 1975), Bale spoke feelingly about the devastation wrought by the Dissolution. He listed survivors in *Index Britanniae Scriptorum. John Bale's Index of British and Other Writers*, edited by R. L. Poole and Mary Bateson, with intro. by J. P. Carley and Caroline Brett (Cambridge, 1990). In 'The Dispersal of the Monastic Libraries and the Salvaging of the Spoils', in *History of Libraries in Britain 2*, edited by Elisabeth Leedham-Green, forthcoming, I have given translations of a number of Leland's observations in *De uiris illustribus* about the monastic collections. Simon Keynes has described 'King Athelstan's Books', in *Learning and Literature in Anglo-Saxon England*, edited by Michael Lapidge and Helmut Gneuss (Cambridge, 1985), pp. 143–201.

Chapter 5: Henry's Reading Habits

T. A. Birrell gives a highly useful and very witty discussion of Henry's reading habits in *English Monarchs and Their Books: From Henry VII to Charles II* (London, 1987), observing, *inter alia*, that 'Perhaps the humble bibliographer can suggest an answer to the historian's rhetorical questions [about what Henry was reading]'. I point out the existence of Henry's annotations in his copy of Thomas Abell's *Inuicta ueritas* in '"A Great Gatherer Together of Books": Archbishop Bancroft's Library at Lambeth (1610) and Its Sources', *Lambeth Palace Library Annual Review* (2001), pp. 50–64. Cranmer's letter to Wolfgang Capito, as Diarmaid MacCulloch has observed in *Thomas Cranmer* (New Haven and London, 1996), p. 183, illuminates 'the dialectical reading methods of a king who prided himself on taking the middle way in religion, yet who had also learned the value of delegation'. MacCulloch (pp. 207–13, 267–8, 308–9) shows the stages by which the 'Bishops' Book' was revised. Michael Hattaway has looked at 'Marginalia by Henry VIII in his Copy of The Bokes of Salomon', *Transactions of the Cambridge Bibliographical Society* 4 (1965), 166–70; as has Pamela Tudor-Craig in 'Henry VIII and King David' (*Early Tudor England*, edited by Williams, pp. 183–205).

Part II Introduction

David Starkey's revisionist and highly readable *Six Wives: The Queens of Henry VIII* (London, 2003) gives a thorough history, with excellent references, of Henry's maritial adventures. Other accounts aimed at a general audience have been written by Alison Weir (1991) and Lady Antonia Fraser (1992). The *locus classicus* is Agnes Strickland's monumental *Lives of the Queens of England*, first published in the midnineteenth century. Retha M. Warnicke's *The Marrying of Anne of Cleves* was published in 2000.

Chapter 6: Catherine of Aragon

There is no up-to-date biography of Catherine of Aragon, and the standard account is still Garrett Mattingly's *Catherine of Aragon* (Boston, 1941), recently described in a syllabus at the University of California at Santa Cruz as 'one of the finest examples of biography ever written'. Maria Dowling has looked specifically at 'Humanist Support for Katherine of Aragon' during the time of her troubles in *Bulletin of the Institute of Historical Research* 57 (1984), 46–55, and Virginia Murphy has probed 'The Literature and Propaganda of Henry VIII's First Divorce', in *The Reign of Henry VIII: Politics, Policy and Piety*, edited by MacCulloch, pp. 135–58. The description of Catherine's visit to the library at Richmond is found in *The Receyt of the Ladie Kateryne*, edited by Gordon Kipling (Oxford, 1990). In *Mary Tudor: A Life* (Oxford, 1989) David Loades examines Catherine's relationship to Mary and prints the New Year's gift-roll of 1557. David Rundle discusses 'A New Golden Age? More, Skelton and the Accession Verses of 1509', in *Renaissance Studies* 9 (1995), 58–76. Janet Backhouse has written about 'Sir John Donne's Flemish Manuscripts', in *Medieval Codicology, Iconography, Literature and Translation: Studies for Keith Val Sinclair*, edited by P. R. Monks and D. D. R. Owen (Leiden, 1994), pp. 48–53. Luther's response to Henry's *Assertio septem sacramentorum* is investigated by Richard Marius in *Martin Luther: The Christian Between God and Death* (Cambridge, Mass. and London, 1999), pp. 339–44. In an unpublished University of London doctoral dissertation, 'Richard Pynson, King's Printer (1506–1529): Printing and Propaganda in Early Tudor England' (1990), pp. 169–74, Pamela Nevile [Sington] has considered tracts which emerged from the anti-Lutheran campaign. To date, the most detailed account of BL MS Royal 11 E.XI, is Janet Backhouse's 'A Salute to the Tudor Rose', in *Miscellanea Martin Wittek: Album de codicologie et paléographie offert à Martin Wittek*, edited by A. Raman and E. Manning (Louvain, 1993), pp. 1–14, but Theodor Dumitrescu has proposed a new interpretation in an unpublished Oxford D.Phil. thesis: 'Anglo-Continental Musical Relations, *c*. 1485–1530'. Herbert Kellman has edited a volume devoted to *The Treasury of Petrus Alamire* (Ghent and Amsterdam, 1999). The postmortem inventory of Catherine's goods at Baynard's Castle was printed by J. G. Nichols in *The Camden Miscellany* III (1855), pp. 23–41; and the letter from Sir Edmund Bedingfield by J. B. in 'Original documents relating to Queen Katharine of Arragon', *The Gentleman's Magazine* 196 (1854), 572–74. William Forrest's *The History of Grisild the Second* was edited by W. D. Macray for the Roxborough Club in 1875.

Chapter 7: Anne Boleyn

The Oxford historian Steve Gunn has described the scholarly debate over Anne Boleyn's fall from favour as a kind of trench warfare. Two of the principal combatants have written full-length biographies of Henry's second queen: Eric Ives's *Anne Boleyn*, first published in 1986 and issued in a much revised version in 2004, is generally considered the authoritative account, and is comprehensive in its coverage; Retha M. Warnicke, on the other hand, considers the possible sexual politics involved in *The Rise and Fall of Anne Boleyn*

(Cambridge, 1989). George W. Bernard has proposed a differing interpretation of her trial and the events leading up to it. As Maria Dowling has observed in *Henry VIII: A European Court in England*, p. 111, the evidence is ambiguous: 'The physical traces of her activity – her books and the documents which show her patronage – demonstrate that the assessment of her friends [that she was a reformer] and her enemies [that she helped spread Lutheranism in England] was accurate.' Anne's precise relationship with Sir Thomas Wyatt and the extent to which his poetry can be read biographically is also a controversial topic: one of the most 'historical' readings is by Perez Zagorin in 'Sir Thomas Wyatt and the Court of Henry VIII', in *The Journal of Medieval and Renaissance Studies* 23 (1993), 113–41. Rose Hickman's description of how her father, Sir William Locke, procured books abroad for Anne can be found in Joy Shakespeare and Maria Dowling, 'Religion and Politics in Mid-Tudor England through the Eyes of an English Protestant Woman: The Recollections of Rose Hickman', *Bulletin of the Institute of Historical Research* 55 (1982), 94–101. Myra D. Orth notes parallels with books owned by Marguerite of Navarre in 'Radical Beauty: Marguerite of Navarre's Illuminated Protestant Catechism and Confession', *Sixteenth Century Journal* 24 (1993), 383–427. The relationship between 'Le Pasteur évangélique' and its French original has been examined by Dowling in *Henry VIII: A European Court in England*, pp. 109–10, and by Eric Ives in *François Ier et Henri VIII. Deux Princes de la Renaissance, 1515–1547*, edited by C. Giry-Deloison (Lille 1996), pp. 95–7. I look at her French books – focusing on BL MS Harley 6561 and Northumberland, Percy MS 465 – and their religious significance in '"Her moost lovyng and fryndely brother sendeth gretyng": Anne Boleyn's Manuscripts and their Sources', in *Illuminating the Book. Makers and Interpreters*, edited by M. P. Brown and S. McKendrick (London, 1998), pp. 261–80. Further details on her possible connections with Simon Du Bois's press will be found in my forthcoming study of 'French Evangelical Books at the Court of Henry VIII'.

Chapter 8: Catherine Howard

The standard account of Catherine Howard's life remains that of Lacey Baldwin Smith, *A Tudor Tragedy: The Life and Times of Catherine Howard* (New York, 1961). I have argued for a link between the KH bindings in the Nottingham bequest and Catherine in 'Sir Thomas Bodley's Library and its Acquisitions', pp. 357–86.

Chapter 9: Catherine Parr

Susan E. James's recent biography, *Kateryn Parr: The Making of a Queen* (Aldershot, 1999), contains full bibliographical references. In 'A Tudor Queen Finds Her Voice: Katherine Parr's Lamentation of a Sinner', in *The Historical Renaissance: New Essays on Tudor and Stuart Literature and Culture*, edited by Heather Dubrow and Richard Strier (Chicago, 1988), pp. 15–47 Janel Mueller gives a feminist approach. She looks at the *Prayers or Meditations* from another perspective in 'Devotion as Difference: Intertextuality in Queen Katherine Parr's *Prayers or Meditations* (1545)', in *The Huntington Library Quarterly* 53 (1990), 171–97. John N. King discusses 'Patronage and Piety: The Influence of Catherine Parr',

in *Silent but for the Word: Tudor Women as Patrons, Translators and Writers of Religious Works*, edited by Margaret Patterson Hannay (Kent, Ohio, 1985), pp. 43–60. E. J. Devereux has written on 'The Publication of the English Paraphrases of Erasmus', in *Bulletin of the John Rylands Library* 51 (1969), 348–67. More generally it is worth consulting *Holy Scripture Speaks: The Production and Reception of Erasmus' Paraphrases on the New Testament*, edited by Hilmar M. Pabel and Mark Vessey (Toronto, 2002).

Chapter 10: The Fate of the Collection

Apart from the section on the 'Subsequent Fate of the Collection' in the introduction to *The Libraries of King Henry VIII*, I discuss 'Monastic Collections and their Dispersal', in *The Cambridge History of the Book in Britain, IV: 1557–1695*, edited by J. Barnard and D. F. McKenzie (Cambridge, 2002), pp. 339–47. I take up the same themes in 'The Dispersal of the Monastic Libraries and the Salvaging of the Spoils', in *History of Libraries in Britain 2*, edited by Leedham-Green, forthcoming. Individual collectors are mentioned in *The Recovery of the Past in Early Elizabethan England: Documents by John Bale and John Joscelyn from the Circle of Matthew Parker*, edited by Timothy Graham and Andrew G. Watson (Cambridge, 1998). In the introduction to the first volume of *British Museum, Catalogue of Western Manuscripts in the Old Royal and King's Collections* (London, 1921), Julius P. Gilson has provided a survey of the royal librarians in Henry's and Elizabeth's reign; further work is being undertaken by Peter Blayney, who kindly drew my attention to Andrew Bright's reversion of the office of keeper of the library at Westminster for life in 1593. I have made a preliminary study of Bancroft's borrowings in '"A Great Gatherer Together of Books"', and I describe 'The Royal Library as a Source for Sir Robert Cotton's Collection: A Preliminary List of Acquisitions', in *Sir Robert Cotton as Collector: Essays on an Early Stuart Courtier and his Legacy*, edited by C. J. Wright (London, 1997), pp. 208–29. C. G. C. Tite has given a magisterial account of *The Manuscript Library of Sir Robert Cotton* in his Panizzi Lectures for 1993 (London, 1994). This is further developed in his *The Early Records of Sir Robert Cotton's Library: Formation, Cataloguing, Use* (London, 2004). Francesco Giorgi's *De harmonia mundi* is described in J.-F. Maillard, 'Henry VIII et George de Venise: Documents sur l'affaire du divorce', *Révue de l'histoire des religions* 181 (1972), 157–86. T. A. Birrell's succinct and perceptive account of *English Monarchs and Their Books: From Henry VII to Charles II* will soon be supplemented by his full study of the growth of the English royal library, and his, I think, should be the final word on the value of a bibliographical study of Henry's (or any other historical) library: 'One of the things we learn in studying old libraries is that it makes us read what interested *them*, not what interests *us*...Old libraries offer the most specific, concrete and indisputable evidence for cultural history, but it is evidence that obstinately resists neat patterns and facile generalisations.'